INST
MEN
TRANSLATOR

FRANCE *Catherine Manac'h*

GERMANY *Hans & Gabbi Jacobi*

ITALY *Simonetta Vigni*

SPAIN *Consuelo de Urcola*

W. FOULSHAM & CO. LTD.
LONDON · NEW YORK · TORONTO
CAPE TOWN · SYDNEY

W. FOULSHAM & COMPANY LIMITED
Yeovil Road, Slough, Berkshire SL1 4JH,
England

ISBN 0-572-01164-4

Printed in Great Britain by
Page Bros., Norwich

Introduction

In this book we have listed the more popular dishes of France, Italy, Germany and Spain and we hope that it will enable you to find out more about Continental cooking and to satisfy your own personal tastes.

The dishes we have included, have been laid out to provide for immediate location. You will see that they are arranged alphabetically and printed in bold type to contrast them from their English definitions. You will also notice that to the left of each dish, the first three letters of its name have been printed. These letters will enable you to locate the alphabetical area you want.

For example, you are in France and looking for **Cassoulet.** Note the first three letters of the name – CAS. Looking through the index initials section, find the pages that contain CAS, in this case those marked **CAS-CHO (p. 8).** Find CAS in one of the left hand columns and you will see the relevant French dishes to its right. The same method is used throughout the book for each country.

You will appreciate that it would be impossible to include every National dish in a reference book of this size. And that occasionally you will be unable to translate all of the dishes offered to you. The Translator will, however, increase your power of choice enormously and certainly ensure greater enjoyment of the cuisine of whichever country you are visiting.

ALO **Aloyau de boeuf rôti:**
Roast sirloin of beef.

ANA **Ananas (frais) au Kirsch:**
(Fresh) sliced pineapple flavoured with a little kirsch liqueur.

AND **Andouille:**
Large pork sausage made with pigs' intestines filled with strips of chitterlings, etc. Usually served cold.

Andouillettes grillés aux pommes:
Grilled chitterlings. Served with boiled or mashed potatoes.

ANG **Anguille fumée:**
Smoked eel.

ART **Artichauts vinaigrette:**
Whole boiled artichokes eaten cold with vinegar and oil (Vinaigrette).

ASP **Asperges d'Argenteuil:**
White asparagus from Argenteuil.

ASS **Assiette anglaise:**
A selection of cooked meats served cold. This usually includes cold roast beef, ham and ox tongue.

Assiette de charcuterie:
A selection of different types of dry sausage and various types of ham and pâtés.

Assiette de crudités: ASS
A selection of fresh, raw vegetables, the best the season has to offer, sliced or shredded and served in a light vinaigrette. (Vinegar and oil).

Avocat: AVO
Avocado pear often served with a strong vinaigrette.

Bananes flambées: BAN
Bananas baked in the oven with sugar and butter. Covered in rum before serving and set alight at the table.

Barbue grillé sauce béarnaise: BAR
Grilled brill. Served with béarnaise sauce.

Beignets de langoustines: BEI
Deep fried scampi.

Belons: BEL
Flat oysters from Brittany.

Bifteck: BIF
See Steak.

Bisque d'écrevisse: BIS
The same as Bisque de homard, using crayfish instead of lobster.

Bisque de homard:
An elaborate lobster soup with vegetables and seasoning, cooked together with white wine and brandy.

BLA **Blanquette de veau:**
Veal. Cooked in stock with vegetables and served in an egg and mushroom sauce.

BOE **Boeuf Bourgignon:**
Braised beef. Cooked in red wine with mushrooms, onions and bacon.

Boeuf en daube:
A piece of rump steak which is marinated and braised in red wine, with vegetables, thyme, bay leaf and garlic.

BOU **Bouillabaisse Marseillaisse:**
A traditional Provencal soup made from fish and shellfish which are only available in the Mediterranean. Herbs, oil and tomatoes are added. This is served in two dishes. One containing the soup and slices of bread, the other pieces of fish.

Bourride provencale:
Fish soup similar to Bouillabaisse but with less variety of fish.

BRA **Brandade de morue:**
Morue is the word for salt cod. This dish is typical of the Languedoc/ Provence region. The salt cod is flavoured with garlic, pounded with oil and served hot with fried bread.

BRO **Brochette d'agneau grillée comme en Camargue:**
Lamb kebab grilled with herbs.

Buisson d'éperlans:　　　　　BUI
Smelt. A delicately flavoured tiny freshwater fish simply fried and piled on a dish.

Cabillaud au gratin:　　　　　CAB
Cod which has been poached and then placed in the oven with a bechamel sauce (milk and flour), covered with grated gruyère and then grilled.

Café:　　　　　CAF
Coffee.

Caille à la sauge:　　　　　CAI
Quail wrapped in sage leaves and roasted.

Canard aux olives:　　　　　CAN
Duck braised with olives.

Caneton à l'orange:
Braised duckling served with orange slices and a sauce made with orange and lemon juice.

Carré d'agneau rôti persillé:　　　　　CAR
Roast loin of lamb covered with parsley and breadcrumbs.

Carré de veau étuvé petits pois à la française:
Rib or best end of neck of veal, braised and served with fresh peas.

CAS **Cassates:**
Ice cream containing fruit.

Cassoulet:
Famous bean stew from the south of France. Prepared with pork or mutton, goose and duck, sausage, bacon and various vegetables.

CÉL **Céleri rémoulade:**
Shredded celery roots mixed with a mayonnaise to which Dijon mustard has been added. Fairly heavily spiced.

CÈP **Cèpes sautés provençales:**
Wild mushrooms, fried in oil with garlic and chopped parsley.

CER **Cervelles d'agneau:**
Lamb's brains, usually served with browned butter, capers and a squeeze of lemon.

CHA **Charcuterie:**
See assiette de charcuterie.

Chateaubriand Béarnaise:
Thick slice of beef fillet, grilled and served with sauce béarnaise.

CHO **Choucroute Alsacienne:**
Sauerkraut cooked in white wine with juniper berries and lean smoked bacon. It is served, heaped on a large dish garnished with frankfurter sausages.

Choux de Bruxelles: CHO
Brussels sprouts tossed in butter.

Civet de lièvre: CIV
*Hare. Marinated in brandy and oil with
thyme and bayleaves and then cooked
in red wine with mushrooms and
onions.*

Coeur d'artichauts: COE
Artichoke hearts.

Coeur de filet:
Best cut of beef fillet.

Colin froid à la parisienne: COL
*Hake. Served cold with diced, hard
boiled eggs, capers and a mixed
vegetable salad.*

Compote: COM
*Fresh fruit compote. Fruit is cooked in a
syrup.*

Confit d'oie: CON
*Goose meat cooked and preserved in
goose fat. Can be served either hot or
cold. A speciality of south west France.*

Consommé de volaille:
Clear soup made from chicken stock.

Consommé vermicelle:
*Clear soup, usually made from chicken
stock, with vermicelli.*

COQ **Coq au vin:**
Chicken. Cooked in red wine with
onions and bacon.

Coquilles St. Jacques:
Scallops, usually served in their shell.

COT **Côte de Boeuf bercy:**
*Roast rib of beef served in a white wine
sauce containing butter, shallots,
parsley and lemon juice.*

Côte de Boeuf grillée béarnaise:
*Grilled rib of beef served with a sauce
made from butter, wine, tarragon,
shallots and eggs.*

Côte de porc charcutière:
*Sauté pork chop with or without
breadcrumbs, served with a white wine
sauce.*

Côte de veau cocotte:
Braised veal chop.

Côte de veau forestière:
*Sauté veal chop, served with
mushrooms and potatoes fried in butter
with bacon.*

Côte de veau Pauline:
*Veal chop coated with a thick wine
sauce, covered with grated gruyère
cheese and grilled.*

Côtelletes de Chevreuil:
Sauté venison (roebuck) cutlets.

Côtelettes de marcassin grillées: COT
*Grilled, wild boar cutlets, usually served
with a chestnut or lentil purée.*

Côtelette de mouton
champvallon:
*Mutton chop baked with onions, sliced
potatoes, thyme and bay leaves.*

Côtes d'agneau grillées à la
provençale:
*Grilled lamb chops served with
tomatoes and stuffed with parsley.*

Crème andalouse: CRÈ
*Tomato purée soup with tapioca cooked
in stock.*

Crème anglaise:
Egg custard.

Crème de légumes:
Clear vegetable soup.

Crêpes flambées au Grand
Marnier:
*Pancakes, flavoured with Grand
Marnier liqueur and set alight before
serving.*

Crevettes grises:
Small, pinkish-grey shrimps.

DAU **Daurade à la crème:**
Sea bream. A very delicately flavoured fish usually served with mushrooms and cream.

DÉL **Délices aux amandes:**
Chocolate ice cream with chocolate sauce and chopped almonds.

ENT **Entrecôte bercy:**
Grilled steak. Served with a bercy butter sauce of melted butter, chopped shallots, bone marrow, white wine, lemon juice and parsley.

Entrecôte aux échalotes:
Grilled steak. Served with butter, chopped shallots and parsley.

Entrecôte maître d'hotel:
Grilled steak. Served with a butter containing chopped parsley and lemon juice.

Entrecôte marchand de vin:
Grilled steak. Served in a red wine sauce with shallots, chopped parsley and lemon juice.

EPI **Epinards frais en branche:**
Fresh spinach. Served whole usually with melted butter.

ESC **Escargots de Bourgogne:**
Vineyard snails. Usually stuffed with garlic, parsley and butter and baked.

FRANCE

Estouffade de boeuf: EST
Beef stew.

Faux-filet moutarde: FAU
Sirloin steak with mustard.

Filet à la diable: FIL
*Grilled fillet steak. Served in a tomato
sauce with parsley and cayenne pepper.*

Filet de boeuf (grillé sauce béarnaise):
*Fillet of beef (grilled with a sauce
béarnaise).*

Filet de brochet beurre blanc oseille:
*Fillet of pike served with a beurre blanc.
Beurre blanc is an exquisite mixture of
vinegar and shallots with butter.*

Filet de merlan Richelieu:
*Whiting fillets fried in butter. Served
with butter, lemon juice, parsley and
strips of truffles.*

Filet de sole meunière:
*Fillets of sole fried in butter. Served
with chopped parsley, lemon juice and
hot butter.*

Filet de turbot au beurre blanc:
*Fillets of turbot. Poached and served
with a beurre blanc. (See* Filet de
brochet beurre blanc *for description.)*

FIL **(Filets de) Maquereau au vin blanc:**
> *Fillets of mackerel cooked in white wine.*

FIN **Fines de Claires:**
> *Oysters from Charentes.*

FLA **Flageolets:**
> *Haricot beans. Smaller and greener than white haricot beans.*

FLO **Flognarde:**
> *A type of thick pancake baked in the oven and served hot or cold with jam.*

FOI **Foie de veau grillée à l'anglaise:**
> *Calf's liver. Cut into small pieces, fried and served with steamed potatoes.*

Foie de veau meunière:
> *Calf's liver. Served with melted butter, lemon, chopped parsley and plain boiled potatoes.*

Foie gras d'oie:
> *Goose liver pâté.*

FON **Fonds d'artichauts sauce hollandaise:**
> *Globe artichoke hearts in a sauce made with egg yolks and butter.*

Fondue Bourguignonne:
> *Fillet steak. Cut into small pieces, fried in oil at the table (by the guests) and eaten with different sauces.*

Fromage de tête: FRO
  Pig's brawn.

Fromages:
  Cheeses.

Fruits rafraichîs: FRU
  Fresh fruit salad.

Galantine de volaille / (au foie   GAL
gras)
  *Boned poultry meat (stuffed with goose
  liver pâté) pressed into a symmetrical
  shape and cooked in a gelatine stock.*

Gigot d'agneau haricots frais: GIG
  *Roast leg of lamb. Served with fresh
  white beans.*

**Gigot de pré-salé rôti, haricots
blancs:**
  *Roast leg of lamb. Served with white
  haricot beans.*

Girolles sautées: GIR
  Wild mushrooms fried in butter.

Glace: GLA
  Ice cream.

Gratin de fruits de mer: GRA
  *Shellfish, served in a white sauce and
  browned in the oven.*

GRA **Gratin de queues de langoustines:**
Tails of langoustines (small type of lobster). Served in a white sauce and browned in the oven.

Gratinée:
See soupe a l'oignon gratinée.

GRE **Grenouilles sautées provençales:**
Frogs legs. Fried in oil with onion, garlic, tomatoes and parsley.

GRI **Grillade sur feu de bois:**
Meat (usually steak) grilled on charcoal.

HAC **Hachis parmentier:**
French version of shepherd's pie.

HAR **Hareng en pot:**
Herring: Marinated and cooked in white wine, vinegar, onions and carrots.

Haricots verts frais:
Fresh french beans usually served in butter.

HOM**Homard à la nage:**
Lobster. Cooked and served in a wine sauce.

HOR **Hors d'oeuvre:**
Cold hors d'oeuvre *often include fish salads, pâtés and salamis.*
Hot hors d'oeuvre *include savouries, sea foods and snails.*

Hure de Porc: HUR
Similar to Fromage de tête.

Jambon: JAM
*Ham. There are a large number of salted
and smoked types of ham in France, often
called* jambon de campagne, de
montagne, de pays *or by the name of a
province,* d'Auvergne, de l'Aveyron, *etc.*

Jambonneau:
*Salt pork. The lower part of the leg
between the foot and the knuckle.
Cooked with breadcrumbs.*

Jésus de morteau: JÉS
*Pork liver sausage made in Franche-
Comté.*

Langouste fraîche mayonnaise: LAN
*Spiny lobster. Boiled and served cold
with mayonnaise.*

Langouste grillées béarnaise:
*Grilled spiny lobster. Served with a
sauce béarnaise.*

Langue de veau ravigotte:
*Braised or poached calf's tongue. Served
with a sauce ravigotte (white wine
sauce with shallots, capers, gherkins,
parsley, thyme, tarragon and mustard).*

Lapin à la moutarde: LAP
*Rabbit. Fried and cooked with garlic,
shallots, bacon, Dijon mustard (strong
vinegar mustard) and cream.*

LEN **Lentiles:**
> *Lentils, usually cooked with small onions.*

LOT **Lotte à l'américaine:**
> *Fillets of angler fish. Boiled and served in a tomato and wine sauce which has been made with tomatoes cooked in oil with shallots, parsley, cherries and tarragon.*

LOU **Loup grillé au fenouil:**
> *Grilled sea bass flavoured with fennel. This is a typical provencal dish.*

MER **Meringue glacée:**
> *Meringue with ice cream.*

Merlan frit et citron:
> *Fried whiting. Served with slices of lemon and parsley.*

Merlan rôti au four:
> *Whiting. Baked in the oven with white wine, lemon and onions.*

MIG **Mignon filet de Boeuf:**
> *Filet Mignon is cut from the centre fillet of steak and trimmed into the shape of a triangle.*

Mignon de veau savoyade:
> *Escalope of veal. Stuffed with ham and gruyère, covered with breadcrumbs and cooked in butter and covered with marsala wine.*

Morue: MOR
See Brandade de morue.

Moules (de bouchot) marinière: MOU
Small mussels usually from Charentes.
These are cooked with shallots, parsley
and a little white wine.

Moules farcies:
Mussels. Stuffed with butter, parsley
and garlic. Cooked in the oven and
served hot.

Mousse au chocolat:
Chocolate mousse. Served iced, topped
with whipped cream and often
flavoured with orange.

Mystère: MYS
Ice cream inside a meringue case which
is coated with chopped almonds.

Noisette d'agneau maintenon: NOI
Noisette is a very delicate piece of meat
taken from the rib or loin of lamb.
Served in a thick sauce with onions and
mushrooms.

Oeuf en cocotte à la crème: OEU
Egg. Poached in a little dish (cocotte)
with pepper, salt and cream.

Oeuf dur mayonnaise:
Cold, hard-boiled egg with mayonnaise.

Olives farcies vertes/noires: OLI
Stuffed green/black olives.

OME **Omelette aux fines herbes:**
Omelette with chopped chives, chervil and tarragon.

Omelette nature:
Plain omelette.

OUR **Oursins:**
Sea urchins, eaten raw.

PAR **Parfait:**
Usually a coffee ice cream, but Parfait can also be flavoured with chocolate, praline or vanilla.

PAT **Pâté de campagne:**
A coarsely shredded meat pâté.

Pâté en croûte:
The same as above but cooked in a pastry case. Usually served cold.

Patisserie:
Generic term used to describe any type of cake or pastry-based sweet.

PAU **Paupiette:**
Thin slice of meat (beef or veal) rolled up, filled with forcemeat, wrapped in thin rashers of bacon and braised.

PET **Petits pois à la française:**
Fresh peas. Cooked with a little butter, water, lettuce leaves and small onions. Peas in France are small and sweet.

Pied de porc grillé: PIE
Grilled pig's trotter.

Pied de veau:
*Boiled calf's foot. Served cold with a
vinaigrette, or fried and eaten with a
sauce tartare.*

Pigeon aux petits pois: PIG
*Braised pigeon. Cooked and served with
fresh peas.*

Pintade/Pintadeau rôti vert pré: PIN
*Roast guinea fowl. Served with
watercress and sauté potatoes.*

Plat du jour: PLA
Speciality of the day.

Plateau de fruits de mer:
*A selection of different shellfish;
shrimps, winkles, prairies (a type of
clam), oysters, crab, langoustine
(scampi).*

Plats garnis:
Meat and vegetables.

Pointes d'asperges: POI
Asparagus tips.

Poireaux (vinaigrette):
Boiled leeks served cold in a vinaigrette.

Poire condé:
*Rice pudding flavoured with vanilla and
decorated with halved pears poached in
syrup.*

POI **Poires belle Hélène:**
*A vanilla ice cream with poached pears.
Served with chocolate sauce.*

Poires au vin:
*Pears poached in wine and served
chilled.*

POM **Pommes à l'huile:**
*Boiled potatoes served cold in a
vinaigrette.*

**Pommes anglaises or à
l'anglaise:**
Boiled potatoes.

Pommes au four:
Baked potatoes.

Pommes frites:
French fried (chipped) potatoes.

Pommes rissolées/sautées:
*Sliced boiled potatoes fried in butter
until golden and served with chopped
parsley.*

POT **Potage:**
Soup. Consommé, *clear and light.*
Crème, *thickened with flour and milk.*

Potage Argenteuil:
*Asparagus soup thickened with egg yolk
and cream.*

FRANCE

Potage Crecy: POT
*Carrot soup served with chopped
chervil leaves and croutons (fried pieces
of bread).*

Potage aux légumes:
Vegetable soup.

Potage St. Germain aux croutons:
*Split-pea soup (fresh peas soup
according to the season). Served with
small pieces of bread fried in butter.*

Pot-au-feu:
*Boiled beef with marrow-bone, carrots,
leeks, turnips, onions. This dish
provides two courses: firstly, a clear
soup made with the stock, then a main
course of meat and vegetables.*

Potée:
*Country-style soup made with pork and
vegetables. Mostly cabbage and
potatoes.*

Potée Lorraine:
*Boiled salt pork with cabbage, carrots,
leeks, turnips and potatoes.*

Poularde/poulet rôti (e):   POU
Roast chicken.

Poularde sauce suprême:
*Boiled chicken. Served in a white sauce
with mushrooms and cream.*

POU **Poulet froid mayonnaise:**
Roast chicken. Served cold with mayonnaise.

PRA **Praires farcies:**
Praires (a type of clam) stuffed with garlic, parsley and butter. Cooked in the oven.

PRO **Profiteroles:**
Little balls of pastry filled with various types of cream; (custard, chocolate sauce, whipped cream) and covered with caramelised sugar.

QUE **Quenelles de brochet:**
Quenelle is a sort of dumpling made with pike forcemeat and bound with eggs. It has a very delicate flavour, and can be prepared in different ways.

QUI **Quiche Lorraine:**
Savoury flan filled with rashers of bacon, eggs and cream.

RAD **Radis beurre:**
Radishes. Usually eaten as an hors d'oeuvre with a little salt and bread and butter.

RAG **Ragoût de mouton:**
Mutton stew (neck, neck chops and breast) with onions, garlic, potatoes and a selection of vegetables. Similar to Irish stew.

Raie au beurre noir: RAI
*Poached skate. Served with browned
butter, capers and a squeeze of lemon.
Usually eaten with boiled potatoes.*

Ratatouille: RAT
*Courgettes (baby marrows), aubergines,
tomatoes, green pepper and onions,
cooked in oil with garlic. Usually served
cold as an hors d'oeuvre or hot as a
vegetable with the main course. A dish
from Provence.*

Rillettes: RIL
*French version of potted meat. Shredded
pork or goose meat cooked in lard and
pounded in a mortar.*

Rillons de Touraine, Vouvray, (Loire Valley):
*Similar to rillettes, using breast of pork,
but not pounded.*

Ris de veau sauté provençale: RIS
*Calf's sweetbreads. Boiled and served
Sauté in butter with herbs and garlic.*

Ris de veau grillé aux nouilles:
*Grilled calf's sweetbreads served with
noodles.*

Riz pilaf: RIZ
*Rice. Fried in butter with chopped
onions.*

ROG **Rognon de veau à la bercy:**
   Grilled calf's kidney. Served with a
   beurre *(butter)* à la bercy.

   **Rognons de veau sauté aux
   champignons:**
   *Calf's kidney. Cut into small pieces and
   fried in butter, mushrooms and white
   wine.*

ROS **Rosette de Lyon (du Beaujolais,
   de Fleurie):**
   *Dry sausage made with pork meat. A
   speciality of Lyon and its area.*

ROU **Rouget barbet grillé:**
   *Red mullet. There are two main types:
   'rouget grondin' and 'rouget barbet';
   the latter, found in the Mediterranean,
   is very delicate. The fish is usually
   grilled (for connoisseurs without being
   cleaned out) and served with butter,
   either 'maître d'hotel' (with chopped
   parsley) or beurre d'anchois' (with
   chopped anchovies).*

RUM **Rumsteack or Romsteck grillé:**
   Grilled rump steak.

SAI **Saint Pierre:**
   *John Dory which has a very delicate
   flavour similar to sole. It can be served
   grilled (grillé) or browned in the oven
   (gratiné).*

Salade: SAL
*Generic term used to describe a green
salad or salad of raw or cooked
vegetables served in a vinaigrette.*

Salade niçoise:
*A mixed salad with potatoes, French
beans, tomatoes, anchovies, olives,
capers. Seasoned with oil and vinegar.*

Sardines fraîches grillées: SAR
*Small, fresh sardines grilled and served
with slices of lemon and boiled potatoes.*

Saucisson: SAU
*Large dried sausage. There are two
main types:*
*Saucisson sec: A dry, lean pork or pork
and beef sausage.*
*Saucisson à l'ail: A pork meat sausage,
seasoned with garlic.*

Saumon fumé toast:
Smoked salmon with toast and butter.

Saumon grillé:
*Grilled salmon. Served with a sauce
béarnaise or a beurre maître d'hotel
(butter with chopped parsley) or a
sauce tartare.*

Sauté d'agneau aux flageolets:
*Lower ribs, neck, shoulder or breast of
lamb sauté with flageolet beans (smaller
and greener than white haricot beans).*

SAV **Savarin:**
Similar to baba au rhum *but larger and in the shape of a crown. This can be filled with whipped cream or egg custard.*

SOI **Soissons au beurre:**
White haricot beans served with butter.

SOL **Sole meunière:**
Sole. Grilled and served with melted butter.

Sole au vin blanc:
Sole. Poached in white wine and served with a sauce made from white wine.

SOR **Sorbet:**
Water ice.

SOU **Soufflé au Grand Marnier:**
Sweet soufflé flavoured with Grand Marnier liqueur.

Soupe:
Broth, A peasant-style soup.

Soupe de crabe:
Crab soup (see soupe aux poissons).

Soupe à l'oignon:
Onion soup.

Soupe à l'oignon gratinée:
Onion soup with bread and grilled grated cheese on top.

FRANCE

Soupe poireaux-pommes (de terres):   SOU
Leek and potato soup.

Steak grillé vert pré: STE
Grilled steak served with watercress.

Steak hâché:
Sauté, minced steak.

Steak au poivre:
Grilled or sauté steak coated with black pepper (very hot).

Steak tartare or Bifteck à la tartare:
Minced steak. Eaten raw with one raw egg, pepper, salt and capers, prepared at the table. (Oil and vinegar optional.)

Steak poële marchand vin:
See entrecôte marchand de vin.

Suprême de barbue bonne femme: SUP
Brill. Baked in the oven with white wine and mushrooms. A flat sea fish with delicate, light flesh.

Tarte: TAR
Flan. A pastry case filled with fruit.

Tarte à l'oignon:
Savoury flan filled with onions, cream and eggs. A speciality of Alsace.

TAR **Tarte au fromage:**
>   *Similar to* Quiche Lorrainee *but using only gruyère cheese instead of bacon.*

TER **Terrine:**
>   *Similar to* pâté. *Usually put into a pie dish (terrine) lined with rashers of bacon and cooked in the oven. There is a wide variety of terrines:* Caneton: *Duckling,* Canard: *Duck,* Foie de volaille: *Poultry livers,* Lièvre: *Hare,* Marcassin: *Wild Boar.*

TET **Tête de veau vinaigrette:**
>   *Boiled and boned calf's head. Served hot with oil and vinegar, salt and pepper.*

TIM **Timbale de homard et langouste:**
>   *Lobster and spiny lobster. Boiled, then diced and mixed with a sauce béchamel and served in a deep dish (timbale).*

Timbale St. Jacques à la Normande:
>   *Scallops with prawns, mussels and button mushrooms. Cooked in milk, fried in butter and served hot with port and cream.*

TOM **Tomates provençales:**
>   *Fried tomatoes with garlic and parsley.*

TOU **Tournedos:**
>   *Small pieces of thick beef fillet, cut into rounds. (Also called medallion of fillet of beef.)*

Tournedos grillés Henri IV: TOU
Sauté tournedos of steak. Served with artichoke hearts, truffles and sauce béarnaise.

Tornedos Rossini:
Sauté tournedos of steak. Served with goose liver pâté and truffles.

Tourteau:
A large crab.

Tranche napolitaine: TRA
Ice cream and water ice in alternate layers, shaped into a mould. Served in slices.

Tripailles / Tripes au vin blanc: TRI
Tripe.

Tripes à la mode de Caen:
Tripe. Cow's stomach cooked in cider and calvados.

Tronçon de bar grillé béarnaise: TRO
A long, narrow piece of fillet of bass served with a sauce béarnaise. The flesh of bass is very delicate.

Truite aux amandes: TRU
Trout. Cooked in butter with chopped almonds and served with lemon.

Truite à la crème:
Trout. Cooked in butter and served with lemon juice and cream.

TRU **Truite fumée:**
Smoked trout.

Truite meunière:
See sole meunière.

Truite aux morilles:
Trout. Cooked in butter and served with a white wine and cream sauce.

TUR **Turbot poché sauce mousseline:**
Poached turbot. Served with a whipped cream sauce mixed with sauce hollandaise (butter and egg yolks).

VAC **Vacherin:**
A meringue case filled with layers of ice cream, fresh fruit and meringue then covered with whipped cream.

VEL **Velouté:**
Shell fish, fish or meat or vegetable soup, sieved and thickened with egg yolk and cream.

VOL **Volaille de Bresse:**
Poultry from the Bresse region, famous for its quality.

How to choose your wine
The wines of France are of the finest in the world and well loved by all Frenchmen. They vary, of course, from district to district; so before making your selection, try to establish which labels are accepted by the local inhabitants. You are unlikely to fare badly by following local taste.

With sea-food and fish a dry white wine
Côtes de Provence, Muscadet (Loire Valley), Chablis (Burgundy), Sylvaner (Alsace), Sancerre (Loire Valley), Pouilly Blanc Fumé (Loire Valley), Pouilly Fuissé (Burgundy), Hermitage (Rhone Valley), Reisling (Alsace), Dry Champagne

With meat light red wines
Beaujolais (Burgundy), Red Mâcon (Burgundy), Chinon, Bourgeuil (Loire Valley), Corbieres (Languedoc)
heavier red wines
Bordeaux, Margaux, Pauillac, St. Emilion, Côtes de Nuits, Côtes de Beaune (Burgundy), Côtes du Rhône, Pomerol St. Julien (Bordeaux), Nuits St. Georges (Burgundy)

With cheese
Soft cheese (Camembert, Brie), Blue veined cheese (Roquefort, Bleu de Bresse), Semi hard cheese (St. Paulin, Cantal)
a light red wine or a full bodied red wine
Fresh cream cheese and goats' cheese
a light red wine or a dry white wine

With dessert and fruit sweet to very sweet
white wine
Montbazillac (Bordeaux), Coteaux du Layon (Loire Valley), Sauternes (Bordeaux), Barsac (Bordeaux)
Sparkling wines
Saumur (Loire Valley), Gaillac (South West), Clairette de Die (South East), Medium sweet Champagne

AAL **Aal:**
> *Eel: abounds in Germany's many lakes.*
> *A highly recommendable dish is "Aal*
> *Grün", so named because of the parsley*
> *and dill used to prepare the white sauce*
> *in which the eel is cooked.*

ANA **Ananas:**
> *Pineapple.*

AUF **Auflauf:**
> *Souffle.*

AUS **Austern:**
> *Oysters.*

BAC **Backhuhn:**
> *Roast chicken.*

BAU **Bauernfrühstück:**
> *Literally "Farmer's Breakfast": a*
> *substantial, rustic meal, consisting of*
> *fried potatoes, scrambled egg, diced*
> *bacon and/or meat as well as chopped*
> *onions.*

BEL **Belegte Brote:**
> *Assorted sandwiches; usually open.*

BIE **Bierwurst:**
> *Beer sausage. Contains lean beef and*
> *pork, slightly smoked and highly*
> *flavoured.*

BIR **Birnen:**
> *Pears.*

Blattspinat: BLA
Leaf spinach.

Blumenkohl: BLU
Cauliflower.

Blumenkohlsalat:
*Cauliflower salad with French dressing
or mayonnaise.*

Blutwurst:
A very superior kind of black pudding.

Bockwurst: BOC
*Boiling sausage consisting of 60% beef
and 40% pork.*

Bohmen: BOH
Beans.

Bouillonkartoffeln or   BOU
Brühkartoffeln:
*Potatoes cooked in a meat stock sauce.
Usually served with boiled beef.*

Bratkartoffeln: BRA
*Potatoes, sliced or cubed and shallow-
fried.*

Bratwurst:
Fried or grilled sausage.

Brechbohnen: BRE
Runner beans broken into pieces.

GERMANY

BUN **Bündner Fleisch:**
Lean beef, salted, smoked and dried. Cut into paper-thin slices and eaten cold like ham. A Swiss speciality.

Bunter Salat:
Mixed salad. Many contain peas, asparagus, cucumber, French beans or cauliflower, mixed with mayonnaise.

CHA **Champignon:**
Button mushrooms.

DAM **Dampfkartoffel:**
Steamed potatoes.

DIA **Diät:**
Diet.

DIL **Dillkartoffeln:**
Potatoes in a sauce flavoured with a herb of mild aniseed flavour, called "dill".

DOP **Doppelte Kraftbrühe:**
Double stength consommé.

EIE **Eierkuchen:**
A thick omelette-type dish, made from eggs and a little flour.

Eiersalat:
Egg salad.

Eierspeisen:
Egg dishes.

Einlage: EIN
Any type of pasta or rice.

eintopf:
Cooked together in one pot.

Eis: EIS
Ice cream.

eisbecher:
*Ice cream served in sundae glass with
fruit or sauce.*

Eisbein:
*Pickled leg of pork which has been
boiled with sauerkraut. Served with
mashed potatoes and pease pudding,
over which some fried diced bacon and
onions have been poured. A hearty meal
requiring lots of beer!*

Entenbraten: ENT
Roast duck.

Erbsen: ERB
Dried peas.

Erbsensuppe:
*Pea soup. A kind of thinned down pease
pudding (yellow or green) with croûtons
on top; often eaten with Frankfurt
sausages heated in the soup.*

Erdbeere: ERD
Strawberry.

GERMANY

FAL **Falscher Hase:**
>   *A blatant misnomer; it has nothing to
>   do with "Hase" (hare), not even its
>   shape. It is simply minced beef loaf.*

FIL **Filetbraten:**
>   *Roast filler of beef.*

FIS **Fischgerichte:**
>   *Fish dishes.*

Fischklösse:
>   *Fish balls or dumplings.*

Fisch-Koteletts:
>   *Fish cutlets.*

Fischsuppe:
>   *Fish soup.*

FLE **Fleischbrühe:**
>   *Consommé made of clear beef stock or
>   at times, unfortunately, of meat extract.*

Fleischbrühe mit Einlage:
>   *Consommé which may contain any
>   shape of pasta or rice.*

Fleischbrühe mit Einlauf:
>   *Consommé, to which a thin dough
>   mixture is added drop by drop.*

Fleischgerichte:
>   *Meat dishes.*

Flunder: FLU
Flounder. A flat fish, most frequently caught in the Baltic. Smoked "flunder" is a great delicacy.

Forellen: FOR
Trout. "Forellen blau" means the trout has been cooked within an hour of being killed when it therefore retains its bluish colour.

Frankfurter Würstchen: FRA
"Wurstchen": – diminutive "Wurst". A thin boiling sausage of pure pork, slightly smoked.

GERMANY

Frikassee: FRI
Fricassee of various meats or poultry, boiled and served in a light-coloured sauce with mushrooms, capers, lemon juice and cream. Usually served in a rice-ring.

Frisch:
Fresh.

Fürst Pückler (Eis): FUR
Semi-frozen ice cream containing whipped cream.

Gänsebraten: GAN
Roast goose. In Germany goose is preferred to turkey as being tastier and juicier.

GEB **Gebacken:**
Baked.

Gebacken Kartoffeln:
Roast potatoes in their jackets.

Gebraten:
Fried.

GED **Gedünsted:**
Steamed.

GEE **Geeist:**
Iced.

GEF **Geflügel:**
Poultry.

Geflügelfrikassee:
Fricassee of poultry. See also Frikassee.

Gefüllt:
Filled or – more often – stuffed.

Gefüllte Kalbsbrust:
Roast breast of veal, stuffed.

GEK **Gekochter Schinken:**
Cooked ham.

GEM **Gemischt:**
Mixed.

Gemischter Aufschnitt:
*Plate of assorted slices of cold sausages;
often eaten with* Kartoffelsalat.

Gemischtes Gemüse: GEM
Mixed vegetables.

Gemischte Käseplatte:
Assorted cheese platter.

Gemüse:
Vegetables.

Gepökelt: GEP
Pickled.

Geräucherter Aal: GER
*Smoked eel. A great delicacy, though
rather expensive.*

Gespickt: GES
Larded.

Gewürzgurken: GEW
Spiced cucumbers.

Grüne Bohnen: GRU
French beans.

Grünkernsuppe:
*Green soup: A German speciality, made
from a particular variety of wheat,
ground into flour while still unripe.
Hence Grünkern (green kernel).*

Grünkohl:
Scotch or curly kale.

GERMANY

41

GUL **Gulaschsuppe:**
Goulash soup.

GUR **Gurken:**
Cucumber. Eaten raw as cucumber salad (Gurkensalat) or pickled in various ways.

Gurkensalat:
Cucumber salad. usually served with French dressing and sour cream.

Gurkensuppe:
Cucumber soup. A delicately tasting cream soup.

HAC **Hackbraten:**
See Falscher Hase.

HAM **Hammelfleisch:**
Mutton.

Hammelfleisch mit Grünen Bohnen:
Mutton stewed together with runner beans and potatoes.

Hammelkeule:
Leg of mutton.

Hammelkotelett:
Mutton cutlet. See also Kottelett.

HAN **Handkäs mit Musik:**
Strong sour-milk cheese served with vinegar, oil, pepper, salt and chopped onions. Rhenish speciality.

Harzer Käse: HAR
*Very strong and smelly German cheese
made from sour milk.*

Hase: HAS
Hare.

Hasenbraten or Hasenrücken:
Hare. Prepared like Rehrücken.

Hauptsalat: HAU
See under Kopfsalat.

Hecht: HEC
Pike.

Heiss: HEI
Hot.

Hering: HER
*Herring: May be "gebraten" –
"Brathering" (fried Herring),
"Mariniert" (marinaded), filleted it may
be rolled around some slices of onion
and cucumber when it is called
"Rollmops".*

Heringssalat:
*Herring salad. Pickled herrings, cut
finely with diced cucumber and apples.*

Himbeeren: HIM
Raspberries.

Hirschrücken: HIR
See Rehrücken.

GERMANY

43

HOL **Holländer Käse:**
Edam or Gouda cheese.

HUH **Huhn mit Reis:**
Boiled chicken with rice.

Hühnerbrühe:
Consommé of chicken. Served either clear or with a raw egg (Ei) added. The latter version is highly recommended as a snack to accompany a vol-au-vent.

Hühnerfrikassee:
Fricassee of chicken. See also Frikassee.

Hühnersalat:
Chicken salad: Finely chopped chicken, mixed with peas and French dressing or mayonnaise.

Hühnersuppe:
Chicken soup (Creamed or consommé).

HUM **Hummer:**
Lobster: Kalter hummer *(cold lobster);* hummer mayonnaise *(lobster mayonnaise);* hummer frikassee *(lobster fricassee).*

ITA **Italienischer Salat:**
Italian Salad. Similar to Heringssalat, *but with diced, cooked meat.*

KAB **Kabeljau:**
Cod.

Kaiserschmarren: KAI
*Sweet, soufflé omelette. An Austrian
delicacy served in small pieces.*

Kalbsbraten: KAL
*Roast Veal. Veal is very highly
recommended in Germany and is
comparable to best English lamb. As it
has no pronounced taste, it is usually
served in strongly flavoured, fancy
sauces, often finished with sour cream.*

Kalbsbrust:
*Roast Breast of Veal. Usually stuffed
(gefüllt), the filling frequently
consisting of a mixture of rice and
mushrooms.*

Kalbsfrikassee:
Fricassee of veal. See also Frikassee.

Kalbshaxe also Kalbscache:
Knuckle of veal.

Kalbskeule:
Leg of veal.

Kalbskotelett:
See Kotelett.

Kalbsleber:
Calves' liver.

Kalbsmedaillon:
*Fillet of veal. Served with various
sauces and garnishes. Very, very tender.*

GERMANY

KAL **Kalbsnierenbraten:**
Roast loin of veal, with the kidneys still attached. Usually served in cream sauce. Highly recommended.

Kalbsschnitzel:
See Schnitzel.

Kalbszunge:
Calf's tongue.

Kalt:
Cod.

Kalter Hummer:
Cold lobster.

Kaltschale:
Collective name for clear, sweet soups, made from various fruit juices, white wine or lager. Normally served chilled, it is most freshing in the summer.

Kalte Speisen:
Cold dishes.

KAR **Karotten:**
Young carrots.

Karpfen:
Carp. Often cooked in beer.

Kartoffel:
Potato.

Kartoffelbrei or Kartoffelpurée:
Creamed potatoes.

Kartoffelklôsse or
Kartoffelknödel:
*Dumplings made of raw potatoes. Very
tasty. "Klösse" is the North German
term and "Knödel" is the term used in
Southern Germany and in Austria.*

Kartoffelkrokette:
Potato croquettes.

Kartoffelpuffer:
*Potato-pancakes. Raw potatoes grated
and then mixed with egg and a little
flour; fried into very thin golden crisp
pancakes.*

Kartoffelsalat:
*Potato salad, with diced apples, and
pickled cucumbers: A very popular
snack when accompanied by some hot
sausage like* Bockwurst *or* Frankfurter
*(see these) and washed down with a
large glass of beer.*

Kartoffelsuppe:
*Potato soup containing fried bacon
pieces, and onions. Rather filling.*

Käse:
*Cheese. Not as popular in Germany and
Austria as it is in most of Europe. Most
restaurants have only a limited choice
of German, French and English-type
cheeses. The German varieties are dealt
with separately.*

GERMANY

KAS **Käsekuchen:**
   Cheese Cake.

Kasseler Rippenspeer:
   Pickled and lightly smoked pork cutlets.
   Boiled in a savoury sauce and generally
   eaten with sauerkraut and boiled or
   mashed potatoes.

KAT **Katenschinken also**
   Katenrauchschinken:
   Salted, smoked ham. A speciality of
   Holstein. Usually served in thin slices
   and eaten with coarse rye bread.

KLA **Klar:**
   Clear.

KNA **Knackwurst:**
   A boiling sausage containing a mixture
   of lightly smoked pork and beef.

KNU **Knusprig:**
   Crisp.

KOH **Kohl:**
   Cabbage. The collective name of all
   edible brassicae.

Kohlrabi:
   A little known but tasty vegetable.
   Similar to turnip or celeriac.

KOM **Kompott:**
   Stewed fruit. Often a mixture of several
   varieties.

Königsberger Klopse: KON

*Meat Balls. Usually made from a
mixture of minced pork, veal and beef
and cooked in a savoury sauce.*

Kopfsalat: KOP

*Lettuce in French dressing often with a
little sugar and herbs. Sometimes served
with sour cream and bacon cubes.*

Kotelett: KOT

*Cutlet: cuts from the ribs of veal, pork,
mutton or venison. Nearly always egg-
and-breadcrumbed then shallow-fried.*

Krabben: KRA

Crab or shrimp salad with mayonnaise.

Kraftbrühe:

Consommé. See also Fleischbruhe.
Sometimes called Doppelte
Kraftbrühe, *simply meaning double
strength.*

Krebse: KRE

*Sweet water crayfish. These are at their
most delicious during the summer –
May and August in particular.*

Krebsscheren:

Crayfish Claws.

Krebsschwänze:

Crayfish tails. See also Krebse *and*
Krebssuppe.

GERMANY

KRE **Krebssuppe:**
> *Crayfish soup. The claws and tails of these delicious fresh-water crustaceans swim freely in a soup which gets its special flavour from the finely ground shells of the fish.*

LAC **Lachs:**
> *Salmon: "blau" – fresh boiled; "Gebraten" – fried.*

Lachsforelle:
> *Salmon Trout.*

LAM **Lambrot:**
> *A coarse rye bread.*

Lammbraten:
> *Roast lamb.*

Lammbrust vom Rost:
> *Roast breast of lamb.*

Lammfleisch:
> *Lamb. Caution is urged before choosing a lamb dish. The animal may have exceeded its permitted life-span of one year before slaughter.*

Lammkeule:
> *Roast leg of lamb.*

Lammschulter:
> *Shoulder of lamb.*

Leber: LEB
*Liver. Usually a great delicacy provided
it is calves' liver.*

Leberkäs:
*A sausage containing a spiced mixture
of liver and fat pork. A Bavarian
speciality eaten hot or cold.*

Leberwurst:
*Sausage made from calves' or ox liver.
Normally served as either a sandwich
spread or fried or boiled.*

Linensuppe: LIN
*Lentil soup. German lentils are vastly
superior in taste to the English variety.
They are brown in colour and are often
served with a* Bockwurst *heated in the
soup.*

Linzer Torte:
*Gateau. This type of cake contains
ground hazelnuts and is covered with
jam and trelliswork of dough.*

Liptauer: LIP
*Cream cheese mixed with salt, paprika
and finely chopped onions.*

Mager: MAG
Lean.

Matjes Hering or Matjes Filet: MAT
*Young, salted herrings. These are
usually served with apples and onions
in a cream sauce or with mayonnaise.*

GERMANY

51

MEE **Meeresfrüchte:**
*Seafruit. Fish of all kind, served either
as an appetizer or hot, in a sauce, as
filling for vol-au-vents.*

Meerrettich:
*Horseradish sauce used as a garnish.
See also* sahnenmeerettich.

MEH **Mehlspeisen:**
*Dishes made from flour. Pasta (noodles,
spaghetti, etc.). May also refer to a
sweet dish.*

MOH **Mohnkuchen or Mohnstollen:**
*Ground, sweetened poppy seeds as a
filling in an enriched yeast dough.*

Mohrenkopf:
*"Moor's Head": a ball-shaped
meringue, filled with whipped or
pastry-cream and covered with
chocolate.*

Mohrrüben or Möhren:
Carrots.

MUS **Muschelragout:**
Ragout of Mussels.

NAC **Nachspeisen:**
Desserts.

NIE **Nieren:**
*Kidneys. Served in a variety of fancy
sauces.*

Nudelsuppe: NUD
*Noodle soup; consommé of meat or
chicken stock in which noodles,
vermicelli or fancy-shaped pasta are
cooked.*

Obstsalat: OBS
*Fruit salad. Made from either fresh or
tinned fruit.*

Ochsenmaulsalat: OCH
*Ox-cheek salad: cubes of pickled ox-
cheek in a French dressing.*

GERMANY

Ochsenschwanzsuppe:
*Oxtail soup: A savoury concoction of
pieces of oxtail, cooked in Madeira
wine. Even the tinned version is most
acceptable.*

Pampelmuse: PAM
Grapefruit.

Paniert: PAN
Egg-and-breadcrumbs.

Pastete: PAS
*Vol-au-vents. Made of puff pastry and
filled with small pieces of meat or fish in
a savoury sauce. See also* Ragoût fin
and Meeresfrücht.

Pellkartoffeln: PEL
New potatoes; boiled in their jackets.

PET **Petersiliennkartoffeln:**
Potatoes in a parsley sauce.

PFA **Pfannkuchen:**
See also Eierkuchen. *Also the name for doughnuts, either plain or filled.*

PFE **Pfefferlinge or Pfifferlinge:**
A wild-growing yellow mushroom of excellent taste. Known in English by its French name of Chanterelle.

Pfefferschoten:
Paprika: red or green peppers.

PFI **Pfirsich:**
Peach.

PIL **Pilz:**
Mushroom. There is a great variety of edible mushrooms in Germany.

Pilzsuppe:
Mushroom soup.

PÖK **Pökelrinderbrust:**
Pickled breast of beef. Usually a very tender, mild and juicy piece of boiled, pickled beef. Delicious when washed down with a mug of beer.

Pökelrinderzunge:
See Rinderzunge.

PRE **Preiselbeere:**
Cranberry. Cranberry preserve is very popular with game.

Ragoût fin: RAG
*Veal, calf's tongue, sweetbread and
brains, boiled, finely cut into a savoury
sauce and served au gratin in a
"Muschel" (scallop shell). Also used as
filling in* pastete *or* vol-au-vent.

Räucherlachs: RÄU
Smoked salmon.

Räucherrinderzunge:
See also rinderzunge.

Rehkeule: REH
*Leg of venison. Traditionally served in a
sour-cream sauce.*

Rehkotelett:
See also Kotelett.

Rehrücken:
*Loin of Venison. Marinaded and larded
before roasting. Eaten with sour-cream
sauce, red cabbage and potato purée.*

Reich: REI
Rich.

Rinderrouladen: RIN
Beef olives.

Rindfleischragoût:
Ragoût of beef. See also ragoût.

Rinderschmorbaten:
See also Schmorbraten.

GERMANY

RIN **Rinderzunge:**
> *Ox tongue. Always pickled, sometimes also smoked; served in a hot sauce or cold in combination salads.*

ROH **Roh:**
> *Raw.*

Roher Schinken:
> *Smoked ham.*

ROS **Rosenkohl:**
> *Brussels sprouts.*

Rostrratwürtschen:
> *Coarse-textured grilling sausages.*

Rösti:
> *South German and Swiss way of frying cooked potatoes with onions and bacon.*

Röstkartoffeln:
> *See Bratkartoffeln.*

ROT **Rote Beete or Rote Rüben:**
> *Beetroot.*

Rote Grütze:
> *A superior type of blancmange made of pure fruit juice (raspberries and/or red and black currants). Served with vanilla sauce or whipped cream (Schlagsahne).*

Roter Rübensalat:
> *Beetroot salad: similar to that served in England or America, but with a little more oil.*

Rotkohl: ROT

*Red cabbage. Much more popular in
Germany than in Britain or America,
and rightly so. Many ingredients go into
this dish such as smoked bacon, sausage,
apples, plums, raisins and wine.*

Rotkohlsalat:

*Red cabbage salad: finely shredded red
cabbage.*

Rührei: RÜH

Scrambled egg. Often served mit
Schinken *(Sliced or diced ham) or* mit
Speck *(Bacon).*

Russischer Salat: RUS

*Russian salad: a mixture of herrings,
anchovies, gherkins, apple cubes,
cooked ham, roast veal and hard boiled
eggs in a mayonnaise.*

Sachertorte: SAC

*The most famous of all Vienna gateaux.
Named after the werstwhile, cigar-
smoking Frau Sacher, proprietor of a
celebrated "Konditorei" (a combination
of pastry-shop and café).*

Sahnenmeerrettich: SAH

*Grated horseradish mixed with semi-
whipped cream, lemon juice, salt and
pepper.*

Salat: SAL

Salad.

SAL **Salzburger Knockerl:**
*Famous Austrian sweet: very airy
dumplings made of butter, eggs and
icing sugar.*

Salzkartoffeln:
Boiled potatoes.

SAU **Saure Nieren:**
*Kidneys. Served in a sauce with lemon
juice. A very popular dish.*

Sauer:
Sour.

Sauerampfersuppe:
*Sorrel soup. Sorrel belongs to the
spinach family but has an agreeably
sour taste.*

Sauerkraut or Sauerkohl:
*Sauerkraut: shredded white cabbage
which is pickled. Very popular in
Germany as a main dish served with
smoked fatty meat or sausages and
boiled potatoes. Also eaten cold and
uncooked as salad.*

SCH **Schellfish:**
Haddock.

Schildkrötensuppe:
*Turtle soup. Better-class restaurants
add a dash of Sherry to the soup which
may be clear or thickened.*

Schinken:

*Ham. The ham used in warm dishes
may be pre-cooked (gekochter
Schinken) or just smoked (roher
Schinken). A simple but tasty
combination is Schinken mit Rührei
(with scrambled egg).*

Schinken in Burgunder:
Ham in piquant red wine sauce.

Schinkensalat:
*Ham salad: cooked ham and potatoes
with endives and mayonnaise.*

Schlackwurst:
Cervelat. Eaten in sandwiches.

Schlagsahne:
Whipped cream.

Schleie:
Fish of the carp family.

Schmorbraten:
Potroast.

Schnittbohnen:
Runner beans, sliced.

Schnitzel:
*Thin slices of meat cut from the leg or
fillet of veal, pork or venison. Often
served egg-and-breadcrumbed and
shallow fried with various sauces and
garnishes. To be recommended.*

GERMANY

SCH **Schokoladentorte:**
Chocolate gateau.

Schwarzwurzeln:
*Salsify; a delicious cylindrical root
vegetable, usually served in a cream
sauce.*

Schweinebauch:
Roast belly of pork. Usually gefullt
(stuffed) with apples or minced beef.

Schweinefilet:
Fillet of pork.

Schweinefüsse:
*Pigs' trotters. Normally pickled and
served with sauerkraut and pease
pudding.*

Schweinekeule:
Leg of pork.

Schweinerippchen:
See kassler Rippenspeer.

Schweineschnitzel:
See schnitzel.

Schweinskotelett:
See kotelett.

Schweizer Käse:
Emmenthal or Gruyère cheese.

Schwenkkartoffel:
Boiled new potatoes, tossed in butter.

Seemuschneln: SEE
Mussels.

Seezunge:
Sole. May be gedämpft (steamed),
gebraten *(fried) or* gebacken *(baked).*

Selleri: SEL
*Celeriac – not to be confused with our
celery. Excellent as salad.*

Senfgurken: SEN
Mustard cucumber.

Spargel: SPA
*Asparagus. German asparagus is longer,
thicker and whiter than the English
variety. If served separately, the
asparagus is not cut on the plate, but
picked up by hand, dipped into the
melted butter or sauce and then eaten.*

Spätzle:
*A type of freshly-made short egg-
noodles. Served in place of potatoes
with stews and ragouts. A Bavarian and
Austrian speciality.*

Speck: SPE
Fat bacon.

Spiegelei: SPI
Fried egg.

Spinat:
*Spinach. Either chopped and creamed
or served as leaf spinach* (Blattspinat).

GERMANY

STA **Stampfkartoffeln:**
Mashed potatoes.

Stangenspargel:
See Spargel.

STE **Steinbutt:**
Turbot.

Steinpilze:
Yellow boletus. An edible mushroom of very delicate taste.

SÜS **Süsspeisen:**
Sweets or dessert.

TAG **Tagessuppe:**
Soup of the day.

TOM **Tomatensalat:**
Tomato salad.

VER **Verlorenes Ei:**
Poached egg "lost in a sauce or a soup".

Verschieden:
Various or diverse.

WEI **Weiches Ei:**
Soft boiled egg (3-4 minutes).

Weinkraut:
Sauerkraut cooked in wine.

Weisskohl:
White cabbage.

Weisse Bohnen: WEI
Haricot Beans.

Weisswurst:
Frying sausage made of veal.

Wild: WIL
Game of all kind – furry or feathered.
The most popular is venison which is
eaten all the year round.

Wirsingkohl: WIR
Savoy cabbage.

Wurst: WUR
Sausage. The Germans are known the
world over as "sausage-eaters".

Wurstwsalat:
Sausage salad: cubes of sausage.

Zander: ZAN
Pike: a highly esteemed wholesome
fresh-water fish of delicate taste.

Zart: ZAR
Tender.

Zerlassene Butter: ZER
Melted butter.

Zungenwurst: ZUN
Sausage containing smoked tongues of
pig, calf or beef.

GERMANY

ZWI **Zwiebelkartoffeln:**
Boiled potatoes in an onion sauce.

Zwiebelsuppe:
Onion soup. The better kind is made in the French fashion, with croûtons and lots of grated cheese.

GERMAN WINES

Germany is the most northerly of all wine-growing countries. The grapes from which German wines are made are not exposed to anything like the intense sunshine that ripens the grapes of France, Italy or Spain. Consequently the grapes are not as sweet and the wines therefore not as alcoholic as those of more southern countries.

The main wine-growing areas are:–

Rheinpfalz (Rhenish Palatinate)
These wines have a smooth, gently spicy flavour.

Rheinhessen (Rhenish Hesse)
Second largest wine-growing region whose products are on the whole more aromatic (try Niersteiner Domthal).

Moselle – Saar – Ruwer
The Riesling grape cultivated on the slate soil of the hillsides along these rivers gives these wines a fresh tingling flavour and a delicate acidity. The Saar-wines have a fruity and the Ruwer-wines a spicy taste. (Piesporter Goldtroepfchen is a good choice.)

Baden
From these most southerly vineyards come full-bodied wines. Famous are their Rosés.

Rheingau
Regarded by some experts as the greatest wine-growing area when the Riesling grape yields aristocratic wines with ample bouquet. Hochheim is the place where the true "Hock" comes from.

ABB **Abbacchio:**
Sucking lamb flavoured with garlic, sage and rosemary, seasoned with anchovy paste.

ACC **Acciughe ripiene:**
Fresh anchovies stuffed with cheese, rolled in breadcrumbs and fried.

AGN **Agnello all'arrabbiata:**
Lamb cooked over a fierce fire with olive oil, salt, pepper and vinegar.

Agnello arrosto:
Roast lamb with garlic and herbs.

Agnolotti:
Squares of dough filled with spinach, beef, garlic and herbs usually served with Bolognese sauce and Parmesan cheese.

AMA **Amaretti:**
Almond cookies like macaroons.

ANG **Anguille arrosto:**
Eels roasted on a spit.

Anguille marinate:
Grilled eels marinated for two days in wine vinegar, sultanas, pine nuts, candied peel, garlic and sage.

ANI **Anitra all'olive:**
Duck cooked in olives and seasoned with onions, carrots, celery and parsley.

Antipasto misto: ANT
*An hors d'oeuvre consisting of various
sausages, salami, hams, sardines, eggs,
olives, tomatoes, etc.*

Aringhe affumicate: ARI
*Smoked herrings usually served as an
hors d'oeuvre with onions, salt, pepper
and herbs.*

Aringhe alla calabrese:
*Fresh herrings simmered with garlic and
hot chilli pepper.*

Asparagi: ASP
Boiled asparagus served with butter.

Baccala' alla fiorentina: BAC
*Salted cod fried and served with a
tomato, garlic and fennel sauce.*

Baccala' alla livornese:
*Salted cod simmered in a tomato and
black olive sauce.*

Baccala' alla vicentina:
Salted cod slowly cooked in milk.

Bagna cauda: BAG
*A spicy sauce with garlic in which raw
vegetables are dipped. A speciality from
Piedmont.*

Bistecca alla fiorentina: BIS
*T-bone steak grilled over charcoal and
seasoned with olive oil, salt and pepper.*

ITALY

BOC **Bocconcini:**
> *Thin slices of veal rolled with ham and cheese and cooked in butter.*

BOL **Bollito:**
> *All kinds of meat boiled together and served with haricot beans, potatoes or stewed cabbage. Speciality of the North.*

BOL **Bolognese:**
> *A sauce consisting of minced beef and pork, chopped onions and carrots and herbs. Served with all kinds of pasta.*

BOT **Bottarga:**
> *Hard roe of mullet eaten with olive oil and lemon or baked.*

Bottarga di tonno:
> *Tuna roe either grilled or boiled and served with oil and lemon.*

BRA **Braciola al madera:**
> *Veal cutlets cooked in butter and Madeira wine.*

Braciola con l'acciugata:
> *Beef cutlets fried in breadcrumbs and served in an anchovy sauce.*

Braciola di maiale:
> *Pork chops cooked in butter and fresh sage.*

Braciola fritta in salsa: BRA
Beef cutlets fried in breadcrumbs and served in tomato sauce with garlic and parsley.

Broccoli: BRO
Boiled broccoli usually served with olive oil, salt, pepper and vinegar if desired.

Bruschetta: BRU
Toasted bread rubbed with garlic and served with olive oil, salt and pepper.

Budino Toscano: BUD
A sweet made with ricotta (curd cheese), almonds, candied and dried fruits.

Burrida: BUR
All kinds of fish cooked in a casserole with chopped onions, tomatoes, walnuts, dry white wine, olive oil, garlic and herbs.

Busecca: BUS
Tripe boiled with vegetables and spices to make a thick soup. Speciality from Piedmont.

Cacciucco livornese: CAC
Various kinds of fish cooked in wine, tomatoes and spices.

Calamaretti delle marche: CAL
Ink fish, a type of squid, dipped in white wine and then grilled.

ITALY

CAN **Cannariculi:**
Fried cookies made with honey.

Cannelloni:
Sheets of pasta rolled with a meat, ham and cheese filling. Usually served with tomato sauce.

Cannoli:
Fried pastries stuffed with ricotta cheese, candied orange and lemon and bitter chocolate. A Sicilian speciality.

CAP **Capitone:**
A fat, tasty eel roasted in large rounds.

Caponata:
Aubergines deep-fried, then cooked in onions, celery, tomatoes, anchovies, sugar, capers, green olives, salt and pepper. Served cold. A Sicilian speciality.

Capretto ripieno:
Kid stuffed with spices and herbs and cooked in the oven.

CAR **Carciofi alla giudea:**
Artichokes cooked in olive oil and lemon juice.

Carciofi fritti:
Artichokes dipped in batter and deep-fried.

Carciofi in pinzimonio: CAR
*Raw artichokes dipped in olive oil with
salt and pepper.*

Carciofini sott'olio:
*Small artichokes pickled and stored
under olive oil.*

Cassata: CAS
*An ice-cream made with various
flavours (chocolate, strawberry, vanilla,
orange, etc.) and candied fruits.*

Castagnaccio:
*Chestnut cake with pine nuts and
sultanas.*

Cavolata: CAV
*A soup made from pork trotters, onions,
celery, carrots, parsley, cauliflower and
potatoes, served with Pecorino cheese.
A Sardinian speciality.*

Cibreo: CIB
*Chicken livers grilled in butter and
served in a lemon and egg sauce.*

Cima: CIM
*Breast of veal stuffed with eggs,
pistachio nuts, vegetables and minced
meat. Served cold. A speciality from
Genoa.*

Cinghiale arrosto: CIN
Wild boar roasted on a spit.

ITALY

caffe CORRETTO - coffee with liqueur

COD **Coda alla vaccinara:**
Pieces of ox-tail stewed in a rich tomato sauce and seasoned with a lot of celery.

caffe macchiato - coffee with dash of milk

COL **Colomba:**
An Easter cake rather like "Panettone" but with crystallized sugar.

CON **Coniglio alla cacciatora:**
Rabbit cooked in wine vinegar and seasoned with garlic and sage. A speciality from Calabria.

Coniglio ai capperi:
Rabbit cooked in a caper sauce.

Coniglio in umido:
A rabbit stew including garlic, rosemary, thyme, onions, celery, carrots and tomatoes.

Consommé:
A clear meat broth normally served as a light first course.

COT **Cotechino con fagioli:**
A type of sausage richly spiced, boiled and served with boiled haricot beans seasoned with olive oil and pepper.

COZ **Cozze fritte**
Mussels rolled in flour, dipped into beaten egg and breadcrumbs and deep-fried.

Cozze gratinate: COZ
A mussel dish from Taranto. The mussels, one half of shell removed, are covered in oil, parsley, garlic and breadcrumbs and then browned in the oven.

Crocchette di patate: CRO
Potato croquettes (mashed potatoes blended with eggs and Parmesan cheese, coated with breadcrumbs and then deep fried).

Crostini di fegato:
Chopped chicken and lamb's liver cooked with onions and anchovy fillets. Served on toast.

Culatelli: CUL
A very spicy ham, pear-shaped. A speciality from Bologna.

Fagiano alla milanese: FAG
Pheasant cooked in a casserole with liver, beef, onions, cloves, salt and pepper, Marsala wine and stock.

ITALY

Fagiano tartufato:
Roasted pheasant stuffed with truffles and bacon fat.

Fagioli al fiasco:
Haricot beans traditionally cooked in water in a wine flask hung over charcoal.

FAG **Fagioli all'uccelletto:**
Dry haricot beans boiled and served in a tomato sauce flavoured with sage, garlic and olive oil.

Fagioli bianchi freschi:
Fresh haricot beans boiled and served with olive oil and pepper.

Fagioli con cotiche:
Haricot beans cooked in tomato sauce with slices of pork crackling. A very tasty dish.

FAV **Favata:**
A stew consisting of butter beans, pork sausages, bacon, cabbage, onions, tomatoes and spices. A Sardinian speciality.

Fave:
Broad beans.

FEG **Fegatelli di maiale:**
Pig's liver wrapped in pig's fat with bayleaves and roasted on a spit between two slices of bread.

Fegato alla griglia:
Thin slices of calf's liver grilled and seasoned with sage.

Fegato alla veneziana:
Thinly sliced calf's liver cooked in butter and onions.

Fichi: FIC
*Fresh figs served with Parma ham as an
hors d'oeuvre.*

Filetto al pepe: FIL
*Fillet steak grilled over charcoal and
served with black peppercorns.*

Finocchiona: FIN
A large salami seasoned with fennel.

Focaccia genovese: FOC
A savoury bread with sage and olive oil.

Fonduta: FON
*A hot dip of Fontina cheese, milk and
egg yolks sprinkled with truffles and
white pepper. Served with toast.*

Frittata: FRI
*Omelette. This may be cooked with
many vegetables and meats. The most
common are:*

Frittata di cipolle:
Onion omelette.

Frittata al formaggio:
*Cheese omelette (usually sprinkled with
grated Parmesan cheese and filled with
soft cheeses).*

Frittata di prosciutto:
Cooked ham omelette.

Frittata di zucchine:
Omelette filled with sliced courgettes.

ITALY

FRI **Fritto misto alla fiorentina:**
*Brains, sweetbreads, artichoke hearts,
boned chicken breasts and slices of
cheese dipped in batter and deep-fried.*

Fritto misto di pesce:
*Red mullet, inkfish, squid, octopus,
prawns, etc., dipped in batter and deep-
fried.*

Fritto misto di verdure:
*All kinds of sliced vegetables and cheese
dipped in batter and deep-fried.*

FRU **Frutta candita:**
*Crystallized oranges, tangarines, figs,
etc.*

Frutta di stagione:
*Fresh fruit of the season. The most
common are:*
ciliegie *(cherries)*, albicocche
(apricots),pesche *(peaches)*, uva
(grapes), arance *(oranges)*, cocomero
(water-melon), mele *(apples)*, pere
(pears), fragole *(strawberries)*, banane
(bananas), mandarini *(tangerines)*, etc.

Frutti di marturana:
*Marzipan paste shaped in the form of
various fruits and brightly coloured.
Sicilian speciality.*

FUN **Funghi alla griglia:**
*Large mushrooms grilled over charcoal
and seasoned with olive oil.*

Fungha sott'olio: FUN
Preserved mushrooms. Stored under olive oil and usually served as an hors d'oeuvre.

Gamberoni alla griglia: GAM
Large prawns grilled over charcoal and seasoned with olive oil and herbs.

Gianduia: GIA
A cold chocolate pudding.

Gnocchi di Farina gialla: GNO
Cornflour dumplings served with tomato sauce, grated Parmesan cheese and butter.

Gnocchi di patate:
Potato dumplings served with a tomato or meat sauce, Parmesan cheese and butter.

Gnocchi di semolino:
Semolina, milk and egg dumplings served with butter and grated Parmesan cheese.

Gnocchi verdi:
Dumplings made of spinach and cream cheese. Usually served with butter and grated Parmesan cheese.

Granita di caffe: GRA
Coffee which has been completely frozen and then broken up. Served with fresh cream.

ITALY

GRA **Granita di limone:**
A lemon flavoured syrup which has been completely frozen. A very refreshing sweet.

INS **Insalata mista:**
Mixed salad including lettuce, tomatoes, grated carrots, celery, cucumber seasoned with olive oil, salt, pepper and vinegar or oil.

Insalata di pomodoro:
Sliced tomatoes seasoned with chopped basil, olive oil, salt, pepper and garlic if desired.

LAS **Lasagne:**
Sheets of pasta arranged in layers and baked in the oven. Between the layers there are various thick sauces (meat, cheese, bechamel sauce).

LEP **Lepre alla piemontese:**
Hare cooked in Barbera wine with herbs and sprinkled with bitter chocolate.

Lepre in agro-dolce:
Hare marinated with ham, herbs, wine, salt and pepper, and then simmered in sugar, vinegar, Marsala and stock. This gives a sweet-sour sauce.

Lepre in salmi':
Jugged hare: hare marinated in vegetables, garlic and herbs, and then cooked.

Lingua in salsa verde: LIN
Finely sliced boiled tongue served in an oil, caper, parsley and chopped anchovy sauce.

Lumache alla romana: LUM
Snails which have first been boiled and then cooked in a tasty tomato sauce seasoned with ginger.

Macedonia: MAC
Fresh fruit salad with Maraschino liqueur.

Maccheroni alla chitarra:
Matchstick noodles served with Pecorino cheese and tomato sauce.

Maiale arrosto: MAI
Roast pork, usually seasoned with sage.

Malloreddus: MAL
Small cornflour and saffron dumplings, served with a very spicy sauce and grated Pecorino cheese. Sardinian speciality.

Manzo tonnato: MAN
Thinly sliced boiled beef served with an anchovy and tuna fish sauce, olive oil, vinegar, spices, salt and pepper.

Melanzane alla ligure: MEL
Sliced aubergines cooked in olive oil with onions, tomatoes and beaten eggs.

ITALY

MEL **Melanzane alla parmigiana:**
   *Fried aubergines placed in a baking dish
   in layers with ham, tomato or meat
   sauce, Parmesan cheese and pepper,
   and then heated in the oven. A
   speciality from Parma.*

Melanzane sott'olio:
   *Aubergines marinated in vinegar, and
   then stored in layers under oil with
   basil, garlic and chillis.*

Melone e prosciutto:
   *Sections of fresh melon served as an
   hors d'oeuvre with raw (Parma) ham.*

MIL **Milanese:**
   *Veal cutlets deep-fried in breadcrumbs
   and served with lemon.*

MIN **Minestrone alla fiorentina:**
   *Thick vegetable soup with slices of
   black bread. Served with grated
   Parmesan cheese.*

Minestrone di fagioli:
   *A tasty haricot bean soup seasoned with
   tomatoes, celery, cabbage, carrots,
   onions and herbs. Served with grated
   Parmesan cheese.*

Minestrone di verdura:
   *Vegetable soup containing all kinds of
   chopped vegetables, pasta or rice.
   Served with grated Parmesan cheese.*

Mostaccioli: MOS
*Chocolate cookies containing almonds,
cinnamon and cloves.*

Muscoli al forno: MUS
*Mussels cooked in a tomato sauce with
parsley and olive oil in the oven. A
speciality from Umbria.*

Napoletana: NAP
*A tomato sauce seasoned with various
herbs and sometimes garlic, usually
served with pasta. This sauce is also
known as pommarola.*

Oca arrosto ripiena: OCA
*Goose roasted on a rack with olive oil,
stuffed with pork sausage meat, green
olives and pepper.*

Ossobuco: OSS
*Shin of veal cooked in a tomato sauce
and usually served with rice.*

Ostriche: OST
*Fresh oysters served raw with lemon
juice.*

Ostriche fritte:
Oysters fried in breadcrumbs.

Pandolce: PAN
*A sweet type of bread with a delicate
orange flavour.*

ITALY

PAN **Panettone:**
>   *A typical Christmas cake with sultanas*
>   *and candied fruits.*

Panforte di siena:
>   *A dry cake with almonds and candied*
>   *fruits.*

PAP **Pappardelle alla lepre:**
>   *Pasta noodles served with a hare sauce.*

PAR **Parrozzo:**
>   *A sweet made of flour, egg, almond*
>   *paste and iced with chocolate. From*
>   *Pescara.*

PAS **Pasta con le sarde:**
>   *Macaroni with a sauce of sardines,*
>   *tomatoes, pine nuts, sultanas and*
>   *fennel.*

Pastina in brodo:
>   *Clear meat broth with small pasta*
>   *shapes in it.*

PAT **Paté di fegato alla veneziana:**
>   *A calf's liver paté seasoned with*
>   *parsley, olive oil, onions, salt and*
>   *pepper.*

PEN **Penne alla rustica:**
>   *Pasta (short and tubular in shape)*
>   *served with a hot sauce containing*
>   *chillis, tomatoes, parsley and garlic.*

Peperonata: PEP
Sliced peppers (red, green and yellow) cooked in a rich tomato sauce with onions. A fairly spicy dish.

Peperoni ripieni:
Large peppers stuffed with minced meat, cheese or ham and baked.

Pescespada: PES
Swordfish stuffed with brandy, Mozzarella cheese and herbs, and grilled on charcoal and then sprinkled with herbs. A very spicy dish. A Sicilian speciality.

Pesche al vino:
Sliced fresh peaches served in white or red wine.

Pesto:
A sauce made of basil, garlic, pine nuts and Pecorino cheese. Usually served with trenette. (Curly egg noodles.)

ITALY

Petto di pollo al burro: PET
Chicken breast cooked in butter. This may then be served with various sauces.

Piccata al limone: PIC
Veal cutlets cooked in butter with lemon juice and parsley.

Piccata al marsala:
Veal cutlets cooked in Marsala wine.

PIC **Piccione alla cavour:**
Pigeons cooked in Marsala wine.
Chicken livers are usually added. A
speciality from Piedmont.

Piccione alla diavola:
Pigeons marinated in olive oil, salt and
plenty of Cayenne pepper, and then
cooked over a charcoal grill.

PIS **Piselli e prosciutto:**
Peas slowly cooked with Parma ham
and diced bacon.

PIZ **Pizza ai funghi:**
Pizza baked with mushrooms, garlic,
olive oil and parsley.

Pizza margherita:
Pizza baked with tomatoes, Mozzarella
cheese, basil, olive oil and Parmesan
cheese.

Pizza marinara:
Pizza baked with tomatoes, baby clams,
mussels, garlic and olive oil.

Pizza napoletana:
Pizza baked with tomatoes, Mozzarella
cheese, anchovy fillets, oregano and
olive oil.

Pizza quattro stagioni:
A pizza divided into 4 sections
containing tomatoes, shrimps, anchovy
fillets, Mozzarella cheese, Parmesan
cheese, oregano, olive oil and pepper.

Pizzaiola: PIZ

*Beef steak served with a sauce made of
fresh tomatoes, oregano and black
olives.*

Pizza romana:

*Pizza with Mozzarella and Parmesan
cheese, basil and olive oil.*

Pizza siciliana:

*Pizza with tomatoes, anchovy fillets,
capers, black olives and olive oil.*

Polenta: POL

*Yellow maize flour cooked in water. It is
then served plain with sausages, game
or cheese, fried or baked and served
with various sauces.*

Pollo:

*Chicken. This is served in many ways,
the most common being:*

Pollo all'abruzzese:

*Chicken cooked in a casserole with
sweet peppers.*

Pollo alla diavola:

*Pieces of chicken grilled over charcoal
and served in a lemon and olive oil
sauce, salt and pepper.*

Pollo arrosto:

Roast chicken.

ITALY

POL **Pollo fritto:**
> *Pieces of chicken dipped in batter and deep-fried. Served with slices of lemon.*

Polpette:
> *Meat balls containing herbs, Parmesan cheese, bread and a little milk.*

Polpettone:
> *A meat roll containing garlic, onions, parsley, eggs, cheese and served either hot or cold.*

POM **Pommarola:**
> *See Napoletana.*

Pomodori ripieni:
> *Large tomatoes stuffed with rice and herbs and then baked.*

POR **Porceddu arrosto:**
> *Suckling pig roasted on a spit. A Sardinian speciality.*

Porchetta:
> *A whole pig filled with herbs, fennel and sausages and roasted over a spit.*

PRO **Prosciutto affumicato:**
> *Smoked ham.*

Prosciutto cotto:
> *Cooked ham.*

Prosciutto crudo:
> *Raw ham, generally Parma ham.*

Quaglie ai tartufi: QUA
*Quails cooked with truffles and various
vegetables. The truffles and vegetables
are then sieved and served as a sauce.*

Radicchio di treviso: RAD
*A wild red chicory with a bitter taste
served as a salad with olive oil, salt,
pepper and vinegar if desired. A
speciality of Veneto.*

Ravioli: RAV
*Square pockets of dough stuffed with
minced beef and pork meat. This is
usually served with tomato sauce and
grated Parmesan cheese.*

Ravioli di ricotta:
*Square pockets of dough stuffed with
riccota cheese and served with tomato
sauce.*

Ravioli di spinaci:
*Square pockets of dough stuffed with
spinach and Parmesan cheese.*

ITALY

ribollita: RIB
*Rich soup made with all kinds of
vegetables, herbs and bread.*

Ricciarelli de siena: RIC
Soft almond macaroons.

Risi e bisi: RIS
*A rice dish cooked with peas and served
with Parmesan cheese.*

RIS **Risotto:**
> *Rice cooked in stock with vegetables, herbs, chopped meat or fish. Served with Parmesan cheese.*

Risotto ai funghi:
> *Rice cooked with a mushroom sauce.*

Risotto alla milanese:
> *Rice cooked in butter, stock, saffron and dry white wine if desired.*

Risotto ai gamberi:
> *Rice cooked with prawns.*

ROG **Rognoni in umido:**
> *Ox kidneys stewed in olive oil, onions, tomatoes, parsley, salt and pepper.*

SAG **Sagne chine:**
> *Noodles served with artichokes and meat balls. A speciality from Calabria.*

SAL **Salame:**
> *A type of sausage made with pork, pork fat, herbs, pepper corns, garlic. Salame varies from region to region, but it always has a strong flavour.*

Salsicce:
> *Fresh pork sausages. These are usually fried and served with polenta, haricot beans or lentils.*

Saltimbocca:
> *Veal escalopes with ham and sage.*

Sarde: SAR
Fresh sardines cooked with olive oil and oregano.

Scampi alla diavola: SCA
Scampi cooked in olive oil with lemon. Spices may also be added.

Scampi allo spiedo:
Scampi cooked on a skewer over a charcoal grill. Pieces of white bread are placed between each scampi.

Scampi fritti:
Scampi dipped in batter and deep fried. Served with tartare sauce.

Sedani: SED
Celery: this may be eaten raw or cooked in butter.

Sfogliatelle: SFO
Sweet ricotta cheese turnovers.

ITALY

Sformato di fegatini e spinaci:
A very light egg dish, cooked in the oven, with chicken livers and spinach.

Sformato di melanzane:
A very light egg dish, cooked in the oven, with aubergines.

Sformato di piselli:
A very light egg dish, cooked in the oven, with peas.

SGU **Sguazzetto friuliano:**
A lamb stew with carrots.

SOG **Sogliola alla griglia:**
Sole grilled with parsley and lemon juice.

Sogliola alla mugnaia:
Sole cooked in a wine sauce.

Sogliola alla parmigiana:
Sole cooked in butter and Parmesan cheese.

Sogliola alla veneziana:
Sole cooked in a parsley, garlic, onion and white wine sauce.

SOS **Sospiri:**
Sweet made of grated almond and beaten egg whites mixed with sugar and then fried in oil. Sardinian speciality.

SPA **Spaghetti aglio e olio:**
Spaghetti served with a sauce of garlic and olive oil.

Spaghetti amatriciana:
Spaghetti with a sauce of bacon, fresh tomatoes and strong Pecorino cheese.

Spaghetti bolognese:
Spaghetti served with a rich meat sauce and grated Parmesan cheese.

Spaghetti caprese: SPA
Spaghetti served with tuna fish and large black olives.

Spaghetti carbonara:
Served with a sauce of bacon, black pepper, egg yolks and a little cream.

Spaghetti carrettiera:
Spaghetti served with anchovy, garlic, parsley, chilli and olive oil. Very hot.

Spaghetti in bianco:
Spaghetti served with butter and grated Parmesan cheese.

Spaghetti alle vongole:
Spaghetti served with a mussel, tomato and garlic sauce.

Spezzatino di tacchino: SPE
Turkey cooked in a casserole with olives.

Spezzatino di vitello:
Lean veal stewed with tomatoes, onions and carrots.

Spinaci all'agro: SPI
Spinach boiled and then served with lemon juice, olive oil, salt and pepper.

Stoccafisso: STO
Dried unsalted cod cooked with onion, tomato, garlic, oil, pepper, anchovy paste and with a final addition of milk. Found in Ancona.

ITALY

STR **Stracciatella:**
A clear soup with beaten eggs and cheese added while boiling.

Stracotto:
Beef cooked for three hours in red wine.

Strudel:
A sweet consisting of an outer layer of pastry stuffed with apples, raisins and pine seeds. Speciality from Trentino Alto Adige.

STU **Stufato di manzo:**
Lean beef stewed with tomatoes, onions and sage.

SUP **Suppli':**
Rice croquettes stuffed with Mozzarella cheese and minced meat. A speciality from Rome.

TAC **Tacchino in gelatina:**
Turkey in aspic served in slices.

TAG **Tagliatelle:**
Egg noodles usually served with bolognese sauce.

TON **Tonno alla livornese:**
Fresh tuna fish cooked in a tomato and garlic sauce.

Tonno ai piselli:
Slices of fresh tuna fish served with fresh peas.

Tonno e fagioli:
*Tinned tuna fish served with haricot
beans and olive oil. Pepper and onions
may be added.*

Tortellini:
*Round pockets of dough filled with
minced meats, cheeses, spices and herbs
served with various sauces: tomato,
meat, butter and cheese, cream and
cheese (alla panna).*

Torta:
*Cake. Each region has several kinds of
cake with various flavours.*

Torta pasqualina:
*A pie made from flaky pastry and filled
with spinach, artichokes, eggs, cheese
and milk. From Liguria.*

Tortino di carciofi:
*Slices of artichokes fried with beaten
eggs and seasoned.*

Tortino di carnesecca:
*Slices of bacon fried with beaten eggs
and seasoned.*

Torrone:
*Almond flavoured nougat. Candied
fruits or chocolate may be added.
Usually eaten at Christmas.*

ITALY

TOT **Totani al prezzemolo:**
*Baby squid cooked with parsley, garlic,
olive oil and usually served with fried
bread and slices of lemon.*

TRE **Trenette:**
*Curly egg noodles usually served with a
"pesto" sauce. (see Pesto)*

TRI **Triglie alla griglia:**
*Red mullet grilled on a charcoal grill
with herbs and olive oil.*

Triglie alla ligure:
*Red mullet cooked in a sauce of wine,
garlic and anchovies.*

Triglie alla livornese:
*Red mullet cooked in tomatoes and
garlic.*

Triglie alla siciliana:
*Red mullet grilled with orange peel and
dry white wine.*

Trippa alla fiorentina:
*Tripe stewed in a meat sauce with
spices, tomatoes and onions, served
with grated Parmesan cheese.*

Trote alla brace:
Trout grilled on charcoal.

UOV **Uova al pomodoro:**
Eggs cooked in a simple tomato sauce.

Uova al tegamino: UOV
  Eggs fried in olive oil.

Valdostana: VAL
  *Veal chops stuffed with soft cheese and
  cooked in oil.*

Vincigrassi: VIN
  *A pie made of flaky pastry filled with
  meat sauce, white-sauce and little meat
  balls. Speciality from The Marches.*

Vitello arrosto: VIT
  Roast veal joint.

Vitello bolognese:
  *Veal escalopes cooked with Parma ham
  and Parmesan cheese.*

Zabaglione: ZAB
  *A creamy sweet made of egg yolks,
  sugar and Marsala wine usually served
  hot.*

ITALY

Zampone: ZAM
  *Pig's foot, from which the bone has
  been removed, stuffed with minced pork
  and spices, and then boiled. Usually
  served with lentils or haricot beans of
  polenta.*

Zucca ripiena: ZUC
  *Large marrow stuffed with minced
  meat, herbs and cheese, and then baked
  in the oven.*

ZUC **Zucchini al pomodoro:**
Chopped courgettes cooked in a tomato sauce.

Zucchini fritti:
Sliced courgettes dipped in batter and deep-fried.

Zuccotto fiorentino:
Rich sweet consisting of sponge cake, ice-cream, chocolate, candied fruits, etc.

ZUP **Zuppa di cipolle:**
Onion soup usually served with grated Parmesan cheese.

Zuppa di datteri alla viareggina:
A shell fish (known as dattero = date) soup, heavily seasoned with olive oil, garlic and pepper.

Zuppa Inglese:
A rich trifle

Zuppa di lenticchie:
Thick black lentil soup.

Zuppa di pesce:
A heavy soup consisting of many varieties of fish, garlic, pepper, salt, parsley and tomatoes. Usually served with pieces of fried or toasted bread.

Zuppa pavese:
A clear soup with poached eggs and fried bread with cheese floating in it.

The Wines of Italy

Aglianico *A red sparkling wine from Basilicata.*
Aleatico di Puglia *A strong red wine from Apulia.*
Asti Spumante *The best Italian sparkling wine from Piedmont.*
Barbaresco *A dry red wine from Piedmont.*
Barbera *A fragrant red wine with a very delicate bouquet of cherry and violet*
Bardolino *A light dry red wine from Veneto.*
Barolo *One of the finest wines of Italy.*
Capri Rosso *A dry red wine from the Isle of Capri.*
Capri Bianco *The white variety from the Isle of Capri. It is light and dry.*
Chianti di Arezzo *A red variety of Chianti with a fresh dry taste.*
Chianti di Firenze *The king of Italian wines.*
Chianti di Siena *Probably the best quality of Chianti.*
Chiaretto *A dry rose wine.*
Cinqueterre *White wine fromn Liguria.*
Epomeo *Red and white are available and both are dry.*
Frascati *A typical white wine from the Alban Hills around Rome.*
Gattinara *A sharp ruby-red wine from Piedmont.*
Grottaferrata *Another white wine from the Roman Hills.*
Inferno *a dry red wine from Lombardy.*
Lambrusco di Sorbara *This is one of the most popular red wines of Italy.*
Marsala *One of the greatest sweet wines of Italy.*
Nebbiolo *A sweet red wine from Piedmont.*
Orvieto *An excellent wine from the city of Orvieto.*
Pinot Bianco *The white Italian Burgundy.*
Pinot Rosso *Just as famous as the white variety.*
Portofino *A dry white wine from Liguria.*
Recioto *A sweet wine from Veneto.*
Riesling *A sweetish white wine.*
Sassella *The finest of the wines produced in the Valtellina.*

ITALY

ACE **Acelgas:**
> *A very popular dish of spring cabbage, boiled with potatoes and fried with oil and garlic.*

Acelgas con leche:
> *Spring cabbage. Cooked slowly in milk.*

Acelgas con tomate:
> *Spring cabbage. Stewed with tomato and served with fried potatoes.*

ALC **Alcachofas:**
> *Artichokes. A vegetable generally taken as a first course. Often boiled and served with either lemon, or oil and vinegar dressing. They can also be stuffed with meat.*

ALL **All-i oli:**
> *Garlic-mayonnaise sauce.*

ALM **Almejas:**
> *Clams. Usually served as an appetizer; often simply with lemon juice.*

Almejas a la marinera:
> *Clams. Cooked in a wine and spice sauce.*

Almondigas:
> *A finely chopped mixture of pork or beef, formed into balls, fried and then stewed in a special sauce: (a) tomato sauce or (b) salsa rubia, a sauce of fried butter and flour seasoned with white wine.*

Anchoas: ANC
Anchovies; often served as an aperitif or as a first course. Fried in a deep, hot oil or smoked over a barbecue fire.

Angulas: ANG
Baby eels. Served either as an aperitif or as a first course, in which case they are fried in oil and seasoned with garlic and red peppers.

Arroz: ARR
Rice. Served in a variety of ways, the most popular being Paella.

Arroz a la americana:
White rice served with a highly spiced tomato sauce.

Arroz a la catalana:
A rice dish similar to paella with chicken, squid mussels, peas and tomatoes.

Arroz a la espanola:
White rice with pork, fish, chicken livers, onion, tomatoes and herbs.

Arroz caldoso:
A rice dish which has a liquid consistency, rather like a stew. Served with lots of vegetables.

Arroz con bacalao:
Rice with dried cod, mussels, peas, tomatoes and saffron.

ARR **Arroz con leche:**
Milky rice pudding, served cold.

Arroz con mayonesa:
*Cold white rice served with either
vegetable salad and mayonnaise or tuna
fish.*

ASA **Asadura de cordero guisada:**
*Lamb and onion stew with almonds.
Served with fried bread.*

ATU **Atun:**
*Fresh tuna fish, which can either be
served baked or cold with tartar sauce.*

Atun con tomate:
*Tuna fish stew with tomatoes, red
peppers and onions.*

BAC **Bacalao al pil-pil:**
*Dried and highly salted cod. The fish is
soaked in water, which causes it to
swell. It is then stewed in a sauce with
olive oil, parsley, onion and chilli.*

Bacalao a la vizcaina:
*After being soaked, pieces of cod are
depp fried and then stewed with
tomatoes and red peppers.*

Bacalao en salsa de crema:
*Cod. Stewed in a white sauce, to which
cheese and cream are added at the last
moment.*

Barquitas: BAR
Boat-shaped pastries filled with
savouries: mushrooms, pâté, chicken or
Russian salad, etc. Often served as a
cocktail snack.

Batido: BAT
A type of milk-shake, flavoured with
either various fruits or coffee or
chocolate.

Bechamel: BEC
The general name for a white sauce
made from flour, butter and milk.

Berengenas: BER
Aubergine. Served either on its own as
a first course or as a vegetable
accompanying meat.

Berengenas asadas:
Aubergine. Baked in the oven.

Berengenas fritas:
Aubergine. Dipped in flour and fried in
oil.

Berengenas rellenas:
Aubergine. Stuffed with tomato, onion
and chopped pork and bacon.

Berengenas al gratin:
Aubergine. Fried and then cooked in
bechamel in the oven.

SPAIN

BES **Besugo asado:**
*Sea-bream. A fish, baked in the oven or
barbecued with butter and lemon.
Served with boiled potatoes.*

Besugo con salsa:
*Sea-bream baked in the oven with
potatoes and a parsley and garlic sauce.*

BEV **Bevarois:**
*The general name for a dessert similar
to blancmange. It can be flavoured with
chocolate, fruits, etc.*

BIZ **Bizcocho:**
*Common name for sponge cake. Served
with a variety of fruits, creams or
sauces.*

BOC **Bocadillo:**
*The Spanish equivalent to the sandwich
but made with "French" bread.*

BOL **Bollos:**
*Soft bread rolls or lightly sweetened
buns. Very often served for breakfast.*

BON **Bonito:**
*From the Tuna fish family. More tender
than the "atun" but served in the same
way.*

BOQ **Boquerones:**
*Fresh anchovy. Dipped in flour and
fried in hot oil. More usually found in
the south of Spain.*

Borrachos: BOR
*Pastry served as a dessert. This is a
light sponge cake, soaked in sherry or
rum and decorated with cream.*

Brazo de gitano: BRA
*Swiss roll sponge cake with a rum and
cream filling.*

Budin: BUD
*A flan. An egg based dish, served in
different ways.*

Budin de verduras: BUD
*Vegetables set in an egg and milk flan
which is served with bechamel sauce.*

Budin de pescado:
*A flan containing fish of any type and
served with a bechamel or mayonnaise
sauce.*

Budin de chocolate limon, etc.:
*A sweet flan made with chocolate,
lemon or fruit and served as dessert.*

Buñuelos: BUÑ
*Choux pastry, stuffed with various
fillings, sweet or savoury, and fried in
deep, hot, oil.*

Buñuelos de viento:
*Choux pastry, fried, filled with cream
and served as a dessert.*

SPAIN

BUT **Butifarra:**
> *A type of salami. Sometimes fried with egg, often served as an appetizer and found in bocadillos.*

CAL **Calabacines:**
> *Young marrow. Usually served: (a) Stuffed with minced meat in a tomato sauce; (b) Boiled and served in a salad with spicy sauce; (c) Fried, or boiled, and served with a bechamel or spicy sauce.*

Calamares:
> *Squid.*

Calamares en su tinta:
> *Squid. Served in their own black ink sauce on white rice.*

Calamares a la catalana:
> *Squid. Fried with ham and onions.*

Calamares a la romana:
> *Squid. Sliced into rings, dipped in flour and fried in oil.*

Caldo:
> *Various clear soups made with a meat, fish or vegetable base. Also used as the base for sauces or stews.*

Caldo gallego:
> *White bean, turnip, cabbage, potato and gammon soup. Very filling.*

Callos a la madrileña: CAL
Tripe. Served as either a starter or as a main dish. Boiled, then fried with chorizo, ham, onions and stewed with garlic and pepper.

Canapes: CAN
Small, open sandwiches, often found in bars, some of them carry very strongly tasting fillings.

Canalones:
A kind of pasta stuffed with minced meat, pate or fish. Cooked in the oven with either a white or tomato sauce.

Canutillos:
Rolls of puff pastry stuffed with cream or custard

Cangrejos:
Crab. Served cold as hors d'oeuvres or cooked in a brandy and tomato sauce.

Capon: CAP
A type of chicken specially fattened and served around Christmas. Prepared in the same way as a roast turkey.

Capuchina:
A very light sponge cake, made of egg yolk and soaked in syrup.

Caracoles: CAR
Snails. Served either hot or cold after cooking with herbs.

SPAIN

CAR **Carne:**
*The general Spanish name for meat:
Beef, Veal, Pork or Lamb.*

CHA **Changurro:**
*Crab meat. Cooked in sherry and
brandy sauces.*

CHI **Chipirones:**
*Small squids. Stuffed with ham and egg,
then cooked in their own ink sauce.*

CHO **Chorizo:**
*A typical Spanish salami or sausage.
Used either as an appetizer or as filling
for the bocadillo.*

CHU **Chuletas:**
*Chops. Grilled or fried and served with
various sauces.*

Chuletas a estilo bilbaino:
*Ox or pork. Fried in breadcrumbs and
then cooked in a garlic and green
pepper sauce.*

Chuletas empanadas:
*Lamb chops. Dipped in bechamel and
fried in breadcrumbs.*

Chuletas salteadas:
*Veal chops. Fried and then stewed in
wine with mushrooms.*

Churros:
*A fried batter mixture. Often eaten
dipped into thick liquid chocolate.*

Cochifrito: COC
Fricassée of lamb with lemon and garlic.

Cocido madrileno:
Rice soup followed by stewed meat,
chick-peas and white cabbage.

Cocochas a la donostiarra:
Neck of Hake. Stewed in garlic and
served with parsley sauce.

Cola de merluzza: COL
Hake tail. Steamed and served cold with
potatoes, vegetables and mayonnaise.

Cola de merluzza rellena:
Hake tail. Stuffed with ham, egg and
mushrooms, then fried in onions with
garlic and finally baked in the oven
with wine and tomatoes.

Coliflor al horno:
Cauliflower. Boiled then cooked in the
oven with a white cheese sauce. This is
usually taken as a first course.

Coliflor rebozada:
Cauliflower. Boiled then fried in egg
batter, usually to accompany meat.

Coliflor reogada:
Cauliflower. Boiled, then fried in garlic
and oil.

Compotas: COM
Stewed fruits; Apples, Pears, etc.

SPAIN

CON **Conchas de pescado gratinadas:**
Fish prepared with bechamel and grilled in a shell, from which it is eaten.

Conejo a la Ampurdana:
Rabbit braised in wine with chocolate.

Conejo guisado:
Stewed rabbit in a white wine sauce.

COR **Cordero al chilindron:**
Lamb. Fried with onions, red peppers and tomato.

Cordero en menestra:
Lamb. Fried with garlic and onions and then stewed with carrots, peas and artichokes.

Cordero en ragout:
Lamb and vegetables stewed in wine.

CRO **Croquetas:**
Various kinds of minced meat or fish, mixed into a thick paste, which is then rolled in breadcrumbs and fried.

EMP **Empanadas:**
A pastry pie filled with seasoned meats or fish, together with onions and tomatoes.

Empanada gallega:
Sardine and red peppers pie.

Empanadillas: EMP
*Small pastries filled with minced meat
or fish.*

Ensaladas: ENS
*Salads of many types, usually made
with seasonal vegetables. Always
served with salad dressing (oil and
vinegar is the most usual).*

Entremeses: ENT
*Hors d'oeuvres. Very popular cold
titbits ranging from eels to potato
omelette. Often quite filling enough to
be a meal in themselves.*

Escabeche: ESC
*Fish. Pickled with carrots, onions and
bay leaves.*

Estofados: EST
*Beef or other kinds of meat fried in
garlic, onions, tomatoes and red wine.*

Fabada asturiana: FAB
*Thick stew-like soup, made of butter
beans, black pudding, ham, pork and
onions.*

Fiambres: FIA
*All types of sausages. Salami, Jamon
Serrano, Jamon de York, Mortadella,
Salchichon, etc.*

Filetes empanados: FIL
*Fillets of veal. Dipped in egg and
breadcrumbs, then fried in oil.*

SPAIN

FIL **Filloas:**
> *Like pancakes, but rolled and filled with savoury or sweet fillings.*

FLA **Flan:**
> *A sweet dessert similar to egg custard and often flavoured with chocolate, orange or caramel.*

Flan de pescado:
> *A fish custard.*

Flan de verduras:
> *A vegetable custard.*

FRI **Frituras:**
> *Fried dishes.*

GAL **Gallina trufada:**
> *A kind of cold meat pâté made of chicken and truffles.*

GAM **Gambas:**
> *Prawns. Often boiled and served with lemon as an appetizer.*

Gambas al ajillo:
> *Prawns. Boiled, then fried with garlic and parsley.*

Gambas a la plancha:
> *Prawns. Boiled then cooked in the oven.*

GAR **Garbanzos:**
> *Chick-peas.*

Garbanoz guisados: GAR
*Chick-peas stewed with onions,
tomatoes and garlic.*

Gazpacho: GAZ
*A spicy, cold soup made of tomato,
cucumber, pimento, bread and garlic.*

Guisantes: GUI
*Peas. Often served with ham or egg
dishes.*

Habas: HAB
*Fresh broad beans. Generally flavoured
with pieces of ham and bacon fat.*

Helado: HEL
Ice cream.

Higado frito: HIG
Liver. Fried in breadcrumbs.

Higado salteado:
*Liver. Fried in butter with lots of
onions, then cooked in sherry sauce.*

Huevos a los cinco minutos: HUE
Poached egg in bechamel.

Huevos escalfados:
*Eggs. Poached in the oven over a base
of ham and peas then covered with a
thick tomato sauce.*

Huevos fritos:
*Fried eggs. Sometimes served with fried
chorizo or white rice.*

SPAIN

111

HUE **Huevos rellenos:**
> *Stuffed eggs. With tuna fish, ham, pâté or vegetables. Served with salad or with various sauces.*

Huevos revueltos:
> *Scrambled egg with mushrooms, ham or tomato, etc.*

JAM **Jamon de York:**
> *Boiled York ham. Used for sandwiches, salad, etc.*

Jamon serrano:
> *A kind of smoked ham. This can be eaten fresh or used for frying or in composite dishes.*

JUD **Judias:**
> *Small beans. These are often stewed with potatoes, bacon fat and chorizo to make a kind of thick soup, which is then served as a first course.*

Judias verdes:
> *French beans. Used as a vegetable first course, when they are boiled and then fried in a little oil and garlic.*

Judias verdes con tomate:
> *French beans. Prepared as above but with a tomato sauce.*

LAC **Lacon con grelos:**
> *Boiled gammon and cabbage.*

Langosta: LAN
*Lobster. usually boiled then served cold
with a mayonnaise sauce. Alternatively,
hot a la Americana in a brandy tomato
sauce.*

Langostinos:
*A type of baby lobster. Served boiled or
grilled as an appetizer or first course.*

Leche frita: LEC
*A thick cornflour mixture, dipped in egg
and fried. Served as dessert with
cinnamon.*

Lengua de buey a la alsaciana: LEN
*A thick stew of tongues, onions, carrots
and potatoes.*

Lengua estofada:
*A stew of tongues with lots of spices,
onions, carrots, garlic and mushrooms
in a thick wine sauce.*

Lengua gratinada:
*Tongue fried in butter with ham and
chopped onions.*

Lenguado a la marine:
*Baked sole and various shellfish, cooked
in a whisky sauce.*

Lenguado a la parrilla:
*Grilled sole. Served with lemon and
boiled potatoes.*

SPAIN

LEN **Lenguado en salsa de uvas:**
Baked sole in a grape and white wine sauce.

Lentejas guisadas:
Stewed lentils with garlic, pork and tomatoes. Usually served as a thick soup or with rice.

LIE **Liebre:**
Hare. Generally prepared in the same way as the rabbit.

LOM **Lombarda con castañas:**
Red cabbage. stewed with chestnuts.

Lomo con leche:
Loin of pork. Stewed in milk or baked in the oven.

Lomo a la manzana:
Loin of pork. Baked in the oven with apples.

Lomo al queso:
Loin of pork. Fried in butter, then grilled with cheese.

Lomo relleno:
Loin of pork. Stuffed with eggs, breadcrumbs and ham, then baked in stock with brandy. Sliced and served cold with potatoes and other vegetables.

MAC **Macarrones:**
Spaghetti. Boiled and then served with different sauces. Usually a first course.

Manos de cerdo: MAN
*Pigs trotters. Served boiled and cooled
with a vinegar, oil, pepper and onion
dressing.*

Mantecados:
*Typical Spanish dessert like shortbread
made from flour, fat and sherry and
shaped into small, flat cakes.*

Manteqilla:
Butter.

Manzanas con camisa:
*Apples rolled in pastry, baked in the
oven and served with custard.*

Manzanas al homo:
Baked apples with syrup.

Mariscos a la costa brava: MAR
*Shellfish. Cooked in a spiced tomato
sauce.*

Marmitecua:
Fresh tuna fish and potato stew.

Menestra: MEN
*Mixed vegetables. Leeks, carrots, peas,
artichokes, etc., cooked separately then
fried with ham, a little crackling and
wine.*

Menudillos:
*Chicken giblets. Boiled with onions and
then fried.*

MER **Merluza a la americana:**
*Hake. Cut into small pieces and fried,
then stewed in a spicy tomato and
brandy sauce.*

Merluza a la marinera:
*Hake. Poached with various shellfish in
a tomato and almond sauce.*

Merluza fria:
*Boiled or steamed hake. Served cold
with mayonnaise and salad.*

Merluza frita:
*Fried hake. Cut into slices, dipped in
egg and fried.*

Merluza en salsa verde:
*Hake. Stewed with potatoes, parsley
and wine sauce.*

Mero en salsa verde;
Pollock, in a parsley sauce.

MIL **Milojas:**
*Puff pastry filled with real cream.
Served as a dessert.*

MOL **Mollejas:**
*Gizzard or sweetbread. Boiled and then
fried with ham and cooked with
mushrooms and wine.*

MOR **Morcilla:**
*Black pudding. This can be stewed with
beans or fried with cabbage.*

Morros de cerdo: MOR
Pig's trotters. Usually stewed and garnished with almonds.

Morros de cerdo con perdices:
Pig's trotters. Stewed with partridge and served with a chocolate flavoured gravy.

Morros en salsa bilbaina:
Pigs' trotters. Boiled with carrots, leeks, red pepper, garlic, tomato and wine. Then fried with onions and ham and stewed in stock.

Natillas: NAT
A soft custard served by itself as dessert.

Paella: PAE
A very popular dish made from fried meats, fish and vegetables which are cooked with rice in a large two handled frying pan called a paella.

Palmeras: PAL
A type of Danish pastry.

Pastel: PAS
The general term for pies and cakes.

Pastel de castañas:
A pie made of chestnuts which have been cooked in milk, made into a purée and mixed with chocolate. Served cold with cream.

SPAIN

PAS **Pastel de liebre:**
Hare pie. seasoned with a brandy sauce.

PAT **Patatas al ajillo:**
Potatoes. Boiled, then fried with garlic and parsley. Taken as a first course.

Patatas a la aragonesa:
Potatoes. Fried with spices, garlic and egg. Taken as a first course.

Patatas con bacalao:
Potatoes. Boiled with small pieces of dry cod. Taken as a first course.

Patatas estofadas:
Potatoes.Stewed with onions, garlic and spices. Vinegar is added after cooking. Taken as a first course.

Patatas a la importancia:
Potatoes. Sliced, dipped in egg and flour and fried. Then placed in an earthenware pot with oil and garlic to be cooked very slowly. Taken as a first course.

Patatas guisadas con pimenton:
Potatoes. Fried and seasoned with paprika and then stewed with meat and chorizo. Taken as a first course.

Pato a la naranja:
Duck. Roasted in a white wine sauce with oranges.

Pato a la sevillana: PAT
*Duck. Fried, then cooked with wine and
vegetables. Served with sherry sauce
and olives.*

Pavo asado: PAV
Roast turkey.

Pavo con castañas:
*Turkey. Cooked with chestnuts,
vegetables and sherry.*

Pavo con mazanas:
Roast turkey with apples.

Percebes: PER
*Barnacles: Served boiled as an
apertizer.*

Perdices en aspic:
Jellied partridge.

Perdices escabechadas:
Partridge. Boiled in water and vinegar.

Perdices estofadas:
*Partridge. Braised with vegetables and
garlic in a white wine sauce.*

Perdices con salsa de chocolate:
*Partridge. Stewed with vegetables, then
seasoned with breadcrumbs and
chocolate. Served with fried bread.*

Pescadilla: PES
*A smaller type of hake. Cooked in the
same way as the* merluza.

SPAIN

PIC **Pichones con guisantes:**
Pigeons, jointed and stewed with peas.

PIE **Pierna de cordero:**
Roast leg of lamb, served with white beans.

PIS **Pisto:**
Stewed peppers, onions, tomato and marrow.

POL **Pollo con arroz:**
Chicken. Served with saffron rice and peas.

Pollo al chilindron:
Chicken. Served with red peppers, tomatoes and ham.

Pollo a la parrilla:
Chicken. Stuffed and served with highly spiced sauce.

Pollo en pepitoria:
Chicken. Braised in white wine with garlic and almonds.

Pollo en samfaina:
Chicken. Stewed and served with tomatoes, aubergines, garlic and marrow.

POT **Potaje:**
A stew made from different beans, onions and vegetables in a bacon-fat stock.

Potaje de vigilia: POT
Chick-peas stewed with cod and spinach.

Povorones:
A light sweet made of flour, fat and flavouring.

Puerros en ensalada: PUE
Boiled leeks. Served cold with vinegar and oil.

Pulpo a la gallega: PUL
Octopus. Cooked with peppers and paprika.

Pulpo con tomate:
Octopus. Boiled and then cooked slowly with tomatoes, pepper and brandy.

Pure: PUR
The usual term for mashed potatoes, vegetables or beans.

Pure de cangrejos:
Crab purée. Cooked with carrots and rice and served as a soup.

Purrusalda:
Boiled leeks with potatoes and oil.

Ragout: RAG
A stew of mixed meats and seasonal vegetables.

RAP **Rape a la americana:**
Monk-fish. Fried and then cooked in a sauce of brandy and tomato.

Rape a la parrilla:
Monk-fish. Grilled and served with lemon and salad.

RED **Redondo:**
Silverside of meat. Can be roasted or braised with the vegetables. Usually served with mashed potatoes.

REL **Relampagos:**
Equivalent to the French eclairs.

REM **Remolacha:**
Beetroot. Usually boiled and served cold in salads.

REP **Repollo:**
Cabbage. Boiled and then fried in oil with garlic. Usually served with boiled potatoes or black pudding.

Repello relleno:
Cabbage. Stuffed with various meats.

REV **Revueltos:**
Scrambled egg mixed with different ingredients. Mushrooms, ham, etc.

RIN **Riñones al jerez:**
Kidneys. Fried with bacon fat, garlic and onions and then cooked in a sherry sauce. Served with white rice.

Rosquillas: ROS
A type of sweet pastry made into rings,
fried in deep oiled and sprinkled with
sugar.

Salpicon de mariscos: SAL
Prawn and lobster salad.

Salsa española:
A very rich sauce made by boiling
vegetables with fat bacon, wine and
herbs.

Salsa vinagreta:
An oil and vinegar sauce for salads
containing onions, hard-boiled eggs and
olives.

Sangria: SAN
Typical spanish drink, made of red
wine, soda water and fresh orange juice.

Sardinas: SAR
Sardinas asadas:Grilled sardines.

Sardinas fritas:
Sardines. Dipped in flour and fried.

Sesos: SES
Brains, often fried in a batter.

Setas revueltas: SET
Mushrooms. Fried with onions and
garlic. Served as an aperitif or mixed
with scrambled egg as a dish.

SPAIN

SOP **Sopa de ajo:**
A spicy garlic soup containing bread.

Sopa de almendras:
Almond soup.

Sopa de arroz:
Vegetables and rice soup.

Sopa de juliana:
Vegetable soup with garlic.

Sopa de mariscos:
Shellfish soup.

Sopa de pescado:
A thick soup made of bread and fish.

Sopa de puerros:
Leek and potato soup.

TAL **Tallarines:**
A type of pasta generally served with a flavoursome sauce.

Tallos de azelga:
The stalks of lettuce. Boiled and fried with oil and garlic. Sometimes served with bechamel sauce.

Tallos de azelga rebozados:
The stalks of lettuce. Boiled, dipped into egg and fried.

TAP **Tapas:**
Appetizers.

Tarta: TAR
The usual spanish name for a tart or pie.

Ternera mechada: TER
Veal. Cooked and served with a mushroom and tomato sauce.

Ternera rellena:
Veal. Stuffed with pork meat, ham, onions and sherry; fried, then baked in stock. Served with tomatoes and olives.

Ternera sevillana:
Veal. Stuffed with green peppers, olives and sherry.

Terrina de ternera:
Cold meat loaf made from veal, liver and truffles and seasoned with sherry and spices.

Timbal: TIM
A type of flan, made with either mushrooms, spinach, shrimps or fish.

Torrijas: TOR
Bread, soaked in milk then coated in egg and fried. Usually served with jam, caramel or chocolate.

Tortillas:
A general name for omelettes. These can be either plain and called la francesca *or contain various fillings like ham or mushrooms, etc.*

SPAIN

TOR **Tortilla montada:**
A "mountain" of three different omelettes, e.g. ham, asparagus, mushrooms. Covered in a white sauce.

Tortilla de patata:
Round omelette made with fried potatoes and onions. Served as an appetizer or main dish.

TRU **Truchas a la navarra:**
Trout. Marinated with wine and herbs.

Truchas con jamon:
Trout. Stuffed with ham and grilled.

Truchas Maître Hotel:
Trout. Baked in butter with lemon, parsley and garlic.

Turnedor:
Rump steak. Normally grilled or fried.

Turnedor a la madrileña:
Rump steak. Grilled with kidneys.

Turnedor rossini:
Rump steak. Fried slowly in fat and served coated with pâté de foie gras.

VEN **Venado:**
Deer or venison. Fried with ham and then stewed with vegetables.

Verduras: VER
A general term for vegetables. Usually boiled and then fried with garlic and served as a separate dish.

Vieiros: VIE
A type of crab. Boiled and eaten as an apertizer.

Vinagreta: VIN
A sauce made from oil and vinegar with olives, onions, peppers and hard boiled egg.

Yemas: YEM
Small sweets made out of egg yolk, brandy and sugar.

Zarzuela de mariscos: ZAR
Crab, mussels, cockles, shrimps, etc., stewed in a white wine, brandy and tomato sauce. Served on white rice.

Recommended Spanish Wines

Tintos Red
Laguardia
Baños de Ebro
Elciego
Rioja Alavesa
Azpilicueta
Rioja Alta
Monóvar
Pinoso
Albuñol
El Tiemblo
Forrent Tals
Lagunilla
Magallonera
Ribeiro
Jerez
de Betanzos
Fuente de Pedro   Navarro
Paternina
Perelada
Rioja
Bespén
Corella
Campanas
Mauleón
Tacoronte
Mancego
Valbuena de Duero
Vega Sicilia
Cariñena
Valdepeñas
Jumilla
Utiel
Toro

Blancos White
Abastida
Montilla

Cerebros
Medellin
Presanl
Medina
Riveiro
Jerez (Sherry)
Diamante
Valdepeñas
Horcajo de Santiago
Mota del Cuervo
Robres
Lalueza
Lanaja
Jumilla
alvariño
el Rosal
Fuencaliente
Nieva
Valencia
Nava del Rey
Rueda

Rosados Rosé
Manchego
Benejama
Albondón
arevalo
Señorio de Sarriá
Burgos
Magallonera
Milocho
Jerez
Panadés
Monovar
Motilla del Palacar
Casas de Haro
Garafia
Taganana